LION COUNTRY:
INSIDE PENN STATE FOOTBALL

LION COUNTRY:
Inside PENN STATE Football

The triumphs and glories of Penn State football as told by lettermen from different eras, 1948-1981.

by Frank Bilovsky

Leisure Press
P.O. Box 3
West Point, N.Y. 10996

A publication of Leisure Press.
P.O. Box 3, West Point, N.Y. 10996
Copyright © 1982 by Leisure Press
All rights reserved. Printed in the U.S.A.

ISBN 0-88011-072-4
Library of Congress Number 82-81802

Photo Credits
Photographs courtesy of Pennsylvania State University, the
Philadelphia Eagles, the San Diego Chargers, the Pittsburgh
Steelers, Michael J. Maicher, Rich Lucas, Mike Reid, and the
Harrisonburg Patriot-News.

CONTENTS

To Rosemary, a terrific copy reader and an even better wife.

I shall be telling this with a sigh
Somewhere ages and ages hence:
Two roads diverged in a wood, and I —
I took the one less traveled by
And that made all the difference.

From "A Road Not Taken"
Robert Frost

INTRODUCTION

The road has changed dramatically since a young Philadelphian named Dennie Hoggard accepted its challenge four decades ago. In those days, you crossed the Susquehanna River 15 miles north of Harrisburg and faced 75 miles of two-lane misery from Amity Hall to State College, home of Pennsylvania State College. The first part of the journey snaked along the north bank of the Juniata River. After 10 miles, you were on the outskirts of Newport, birthplace and hometown of Billy Cox, one of the Brooklyn Dodger Boys of Summer and one of the all-time great defensive third basemen in baseball history. In his prime, Cox stopped everything at the hot corner.

Twenty miles later, the hot corner was in Mifflintown. There a red light allowed equal time for east-west and north-south traffic. On football Saturdays, the morning traffic headed for the stadium and the evening traffic trying to get back home would back up for miles because the light was never adjusted to allow for the imbalance. The light stopped autos the way Cox used to stop grounders. It was the corner where the tempers got hot.

Ten miles after that, the Juniata took a southwest turn; the road to Penn State bent to the northeast. The next obstacle to be overcome was Seven Mountains, part of the Allegheny range. Find yourself behind a coal truck going up the mountain and your progress seemed even slower than at the Mifflintown traffic light. Finally, the historic Eutaw House in Potters Mills signalled to you that the worst was over. The last 15 miles were in Nittany Valley, past Tusseyville and through Boalsburg and—finally!—Lion Country.

The road—U.S. 322—has bowed to progress somewhat over the years. First the section between Amity Hall and Newport was transformed to four-lane limited accessibility. The luxury was extended to just east of Thompsontown. There already had been added a bypass around Lewistown and a new four-lane strip up the east side of Seven Mountains that allowed gas-guzzlers with eight cylinders to blow exhaust at heavy-duty trucks.

And finally—miracle of miracles!—the red light at Mifflintown was skirted when the new road was extended to two miles beyond Saturday's hot corner. But the last eight mile stretch between that point and Lewistown has never been completed. The work has been scrubbed from the Pennsylvania Department of Transportation's future file. And so now the bottleneck where two lanes become one serves the same purpose as the hated traffic light once did.

Richard Thornburg's people put a sign up at the bottleneck when Penn State was unsuccessfully seeking a national championship and Thornburg was successfully seeking the governorship of Pennsylvania in 1978. The message was terrifically effective for all those automobiles passing by at a turtle's pace. "If Dick Thornburg were governor," the sign read, "this bottleneck wouldn't be here."

Four years later, the governor was formulating his campaign for re-election. The bottleneck was still there.

Maybe the road symbolizes the program. Since 1947, when a combination of war-scarred veterans and kids freshly removed from high school took the Nittany Lions to an undefeated regular season and a tie with Doan Walker and SMU in the Cotton Bowl, to these days when Joe Paterno and his splendid band of recruits make it to bowl every year, lots of things have changed.

Like the location and size of the stadium, for example. Not the stadium itself, just its location and size. Until 1959, the all-steel structure that seated less than 30,000 was on the busiest part of the campus, a decent forward pass from the ancient Nittany Lion Inn and Recreation Hall, home of the basketball, wrestling and gymnastics teams. But after the 1959 season, the stadium (then called Beaver Field) was dismantled into 700 pieces and moved one mile east where the open fields could serve as huge parking lots. And over the last two decades, the capacity of Beaver Stadium has been increased from 46,000 to 83,000.

The school has gone from college to university status. The football program has gone from decent Eastern representative, to national curiosity, to national power. But the Class of '42 alum can feel like he never left as he grabs a sandwich at the Corner room (at College Ave. and Allen St.) or indulges in a toasted sticky bun at the Penn State Diner half a block away.

It is a school and a football program and a town that tend to grab a philosophy—"The only constant is change; the more things change, the more they remain the same"—and prove it so.

This book deals with 11 lives that have been very important to the history of Penn State football in its golden years under coaches Bob Higgins, Joe Bedenk, Rip Engle and Joe Paterno. Some blazed trails, others have endured physical and emotional trials. And all have helped a program that has constantly maintained a Mr. Clean image.

Frank Bilovsky
Cherry Hill, N.J.

One All-American paves the way for another . . . Dave Robinson gets ready to block for Roger Kochman.

1
ROGER KOCHMAN

The receptionist at the Bell of Pennsylvania tower in the shadow of Philadelphia's City Hall hung up the phone and said that Mr. Kochman would be right down to escort me to his office. The feeling was of suspense and intrigue. Roger Kochman, who had been an All-American running back at Penn State in 1962, had undergone an awful injury the following year in his rookie season in the American Football League. The details were sketchy in the mind except that it has something to do with a leg and that Roger had gone back to Penn State to get his master's degree and the whispers around town in the mid-1960's were that Kochman would be a cripple for life.

Would he exit the elevator in a wheelchair, I wondered. Perhaps a cane? But the doors opened and Kochman walked unaided toward me. We shook hands and the first thing that impressed me were the steely, piercing eyes in the middle of the chiseled Germanic face. In another age, I thought, this would have been the perfect Prussian general.

Roger Kochman's job with Bell Telephone of Pennsylvania takes him beneath the shadow of Philadelphia's City Hall five days a week. (Photo by Michael J. Maicher)

The walk was very erect. Another military comparison, I thought. It wasn't until we got to Kochman's office that I was to realize the stiff-backed look was the result of the pro football injury that nearly cost Roger his right leg.

Roger Kochman lives with physical pain, which seemed to follow his football career the way a tax collector stalks a scofflaw—even when he isn't in view, his presence can be felt. The sport has hurt him deeply in a physical sense, but he refuses to make the emotional repayment. He still loves to watch the game. Since he came to Philadelphia from Pittsburgh in 1976, he had held season tickets to the Eagles. If his eight-year-old son, Douglas, wants to play football, he will raise no objection.

"I've always been a competitor, enjoyed all kinds of athletics," Kochman explains from behind a well-kept desk and beneath a head of well-groomed greying hair. "I would think my only bad experiences with football revolved around injuries. I played organized football from the time I was eight years old; I was always a running back and I was consistently plagued by a series of nagging injuries. Pulled hamstrings, pulled groin muscles, twisted ankles and separated shoulders. That's the aggravating part of the whole thing and that's what I would call the unpleasant experiences. It's a brutal game, and it's painful, but I kept coming back to it. A basic masochist, I guess.

"But I got a lot of personal satisfaction, not only out of competing but because I was fortunate enough to be successful at it. One of the things I always had a great deal of difficulty understanding were the guys who were on the teams and who essentially went through the same kind of practice sessions and scrimmages and never even got into the game, much less experienced some success at it. I kept looking at them and saying, 'God, why do they do this?' Maybe for the same reasons as I did, I guess, but I think I would have been discouraged if I hadn't had my measure of success."

Success debated injury throughout Kochman's career and both could claim victories. Coming out of Wilkinsburg High in suburban Pittsburgh, Roger was a college coach's dream—an excellent student with good size and the kind of speed that could turn a game around in a hurry. If Woody Hayes' offense was three yards and a cloud of dust, Roger Kochman's potential was 60 yards and a bunch of armfuls of empty air.

Not only that. He had excellent hands. Get him the ball in the flat in a one-on-one situation and start counting to six real quick. And, by God, wasn't it a plus that you didn't have to teach **him** to count to six before you sent him off to Math 101?

So lots of college coaches came courting. Kochman weighed the plusses and minuses and narrowed his choice to three—Pitt, Michigan and Penn State.

"I knew when I was getting recruited, the number of scholarships that Penn State offered were really few in relation to a lot of the other universities," Kochman remembered. "I can recall having my eyes opened going up to the University of Michigan and looking at a picture of their freshman team. It had 110 people on it. When I went to Penn State, I think we had in the neighborhood of 20 grant-in-aids, so I think Penn State had to be very selective when it offered scholarships.

"I was recruited by Joe Paterno. And since then, I've seen that what they recruit are not only good athletes but essentially well-rounded people. The vast majority of them are good students. They're not recruiting en-masse; they are selective in what they are doing. Obviously they have been either lucky or good in getting the talent they've massed. Or both.

"The thing that impressed me and impressed my family about Joe was that he sincerely had my best interest at heart. His advice to me was that if I didn't go to Penn State, he thought I would be better off going to Michigan. He said it had nothing to do with Pitt being a competitor, just that he thought I, personally, would be better off going to Michigan. Which is interesting, because when I made my initial selection, I went for Pitt.

"The reason for that was not only was I from Wilkinsburg, which was close to the Pitt campus, but Pitt's assistant backfield coach at the time—I think it was Vic Fusia—happened to live about half a block away. There was that added kind of impression. I was kind of a shy individual in high school and I'm sure that entered into it; you know, staying-close-to-home kind of syndrome rather than going out to the big bad world of Michigan or up to that funny place called University Park which is out in the country someplace. But eventually it seemed to me that I had made the wrong decision and I opted for Penn State, which today I think was a very good decision. I was satisfied not only with the football program, but academically I fared very well. And I believe even the social climate was good for me."

And the athletic climate was fine, except for those annoying injuries. Roger played sparingly his sophomore year, hurt his knee late in the season, missed the season finale against Pitt, then played in the first Liberty Bowl game at frozen Philadelphia Municipal (later JFK) Stadium "in a somewhat limited capacity. My leg was far from being normal."

Despite that and despite the fact that quarterback Richie Lucas was hobbled by a hip pointer, Penn State won over Alabama, 7-0, before 36,211 polar bears disguised as humans. The winning play came late in the first half after a pathetic Alabama four-yard punt gave the ball to Penn State at the Crimson Tide 22. Galen Hall was the Lion quarterback. A pass gained four yards and Rip Engle sent in a fake field goal. The ball was snapped to apparent holder Hall with a second on the clock, Galen rolled to his right, then threw the ball against the grain to his left to a reserve running back who picked his spots behind his blockers and dove into the end zone with the only touchdown of the game.

The running back was gimpy-legged sophomore Roger Kochman.

Penn State returned to the Liberty Bowl the following year and decimated Oregon, 41-12, but Roger didn't play. He had torn up his knee the previous baseball season and had to sit out the entire season. The next two years made up for it, however. As a junior in 1961, he finally got to play against his original college choice, Pitt, and helped the Nittany Lions club the Panthers, 47-26, to conclude a 7-3 season that became even better with a 30-15 victory over Georgia Tech in the Gator Bowl. He ran for 666 yards and a 5.2 regular season average and scored nine touchdowns (six rushing, three on passes). Then, in the Gator Bowl, he gained 76 yards in 13 carries, caught two passes for 36 yards and teamed up with Hall again for a 32-yard TD strike.

His senior year he was named an All-American by the Coaches Association after gaining 652 yards, at 5.4 a crack. His eight touchdowns were equally divided between rushes and catches. And then came a second trip to the Gator Bowl and the bitter aftertaste to a college career laced with carob.

"The 1962 Gator Bowl was disgusting," Kochman said two decades after the fact. "It had to be one of the biggest disappointments I ever had because I thought we had an excellent team (9-1 in the regular season with only a three-point loss to Army). There were Bob Mitinger, Dave Robinson, myself; Galen Hall was the quarterback, Glenn Ressler was a sophomore. Charlie Sieminski was a tackle who was drafted by the 49ers. Harrison Rosdahl was drafted by the pros. Dave Hayes, who was the fullback, was drafted."

Kochman had been drafted the previous year by the American League Buffalo Bills and the National League St. Louis Cardinals as a future pick—a fourth year player who was medically redshirted for one season and therefore still had a year of eligibility remaining.

The ground rules were simple: Sign the future pick before the following draft and he's yours. The tactics were complex, something taken out of a manual of guerilla warfare. Stash the prospect in a motel, if possible, far away from the enemy. If the enemy can't find him, the enemy can't sign him. After all, this was war and war is hell.

For Penn State and Roger Kochman, so was the 1962 Gator Bowl.

"What was happening at the time—well, I hate to use the word interference, so let's just say that there was pressure from the pro teams trying to sign guys to contracts," Kochman said. "I know personally that Dave Robinson and I were both very much involved in that. It made it very difficult to concentrate on the game. You found yourself as a young person looking at what was a substantial amount of dollars at the time and saying to yourself, 'Do I want to play in this game? I might get hurt! And I don't think (opponent) Florida was in the same situation. I think they had a relatively young team. But we did not play well and it was a very big disappointment. And I can remember right after the game that Rip Engle, Dave Robinson and I had to leave almost immediately to fly to the Hula Bowl. And boy! You talk about a downer, going from Jacksonville to Chicago to San Francisco to Hawaii in what was a direct flight. You are talking about the doldrums."

Although he managed to put decent rushing stats on the post-game sheet with 51 yards in six carries, the Lions lost to Florida, 17-7, and neither the coach nor the two seniors told many jokes above the Pacific.

While Kochman's senior year may have ended in the doldrums, the Nittany Lion program was definitely out of the dormant stage. The vapid era of good records and no bowl bids between the 1948 Cotton Bowl and the 1959 Liberty Bowl had now been watered by four straight post-season appearances. But the seeds of dreaming of a national championship had not yet even been planted.

"When I was there, Penn State was probably more a wrestling and gymnastics school than football," Roger said. "Football had a relatively low profile at that point in time. I can't remember the idea of a national championship ever getting into any of the conversations that we ever had. I think the only time we really entertained those thoughts was my senior year when we were ranked something like third in the country going into a game at West Point. And we lost, 9-6. That was a downer. We went up there with our game plan—we would run the ball down their throats because we outweighed them by something like 30 pounds a man. They came out in a nine-man line. I always tell people that was one of the best games I ever had getting back to the line of scrimmage.

"But even in 1969, going into the Syracuse game, I can't remember us entertaining thoughts of the national championship, though it had to be in the subconscious somewhere with Syracuse being ranked number one and us being undefeated. But we would end up getting edged out (20-18). And I think we blew a national ranking that year because we lost the Pitt game. No, the national championship was never really a drive, never an objective."

It would later become a real objective—some might say a campus obsession—in the Joe Paterno years, but at the time Joe was an assistant, getting ready to run the show under Rip Engle's watchful eye.

"Rip was the kind of guy you couldn't help but like," Roger said. "Rip was almost a father figure to most of the players. He's one of the most understanding people you could ever run into. He very rarely lost his temper. He was under control and he obviously enjoyed what he was doing. A very fine man. He was what he was and he didn't have to apologize for it.

"Even when I was there, Rip was sort of moving toward the background. Joe ran the offense, and going from there is kind of a natural progression. The assistants were all super people. I enjoy going back there to see them again because they haven't changed. Just fine people.

"Joe Paterno, I think, always had a tendency to go with his strengths and, as a result, developed a predictability that opposing coaches took advantage of. And I think the game we lost at West Point against the nine-man line was an indication of that style because I can remember Pete Liske, who was our quarterback, and I going over to Joe and saying, 'Hey, Joe, we've got to open this up. We're getting mauled.' and Joe said it wasn't in our game plan and we hadn't practiced it.

"I can't remember us throwing more than five passes in that game. We had played together as a team for more than two years and, if nothing else, I could have flared out of the backfield and I knew there was no way those inside people were going to cover me 20-30 yards downfield. But Joe was a believer in the fact that you develop a game plan and you just execute. That's the way he lived. Joe tends to stick with those things and those people who have been successful."

And it is hard to argue with Paterno's success, although many Penn State followers believe that it was exactly the predictability that Kochman pointed out in the 1962 Army game that cost the Nittany Lions the 1978 national championship when the offense couldn't gain two feet in two inside plays against Alabama in the Sugar Bowl.

Even more memorable was the 1981 game at Beaver Stadium against Alabama when Penn State needed a touchdown to get into the contest early in the second half after Bear Bryant's strategy of throwing long passes had disrupted State's defense before intermission, something the Bear had discovered and used against the Lions ever since the 1959 Liberty Bowl shutout. Eight plays after the first-and-goal, Alabama found itself with the ball and first-and-99. A pass-interference play had given Penn State seven other chances to punch home the necessary touchdown. Every play went inside. By the time Todd Blackledge lined up for play number eight, former Arkansas coach Frank Broyles was screaming on national TV, "Please run a quarterback option." Apparently Paterno finally realized that he was becoming predictable. Two games later, against Pitt, he exorcised the moths from his playbook and deprived Pitt of a probable national championship in a most humiliating manner, 48-14.

For Roger Kochman, sitting in front of a television set in Havertown, Pa., watching that happen was fun. So was seeing his alma mater tie a Blue and White rope around the midsection of Marcus Allen in the ensuing Fiesta Bowl. And, looking back, he still can remember when football ceased being total fun at the playing level—and then almost became fun again.

It began the summer after the quiet plane ride from the disaster in Jacksonville to Hawaii. This time, the plane would fly to Chicago and the bus would lead to Soldier Field.

"Going into the College All-Star game, I was not in shape," Kochman said. "And they played me at fullback, which I had never played. From there, I went up to the Buffalo Bills' training camp and they tried to use me at split end. That was probably the first time in my life that I had ever been out of shape. For the first time that I can remember, I had taken off a couple of months to relax. My weight went up. I just wasn't ready to play football at that point.

"I think it probably was because I was starting a new stage. I had gone from age eight to age 21 basically working out in some capacity every day. I think once that stage was over I subconsciously said, 'Hell, I deserve a rest.' And I think that may be true because a lot of the fun had gone out of football. Now it was a job. Even the last year at Penn State had taken on more of the job connotation. When I got hurt my sophomore year and then stepped in a hole that summer playing baseball and ripped my knee cartilage and sat out the next year, from that point on, the fun kind of went out of it because every game, every practice, I had to have my knee severely taped. It limited my mobility and limited my speed. As a consequence, I had to play a different style of football. I was not a power runner up to then, I was a speed runner. But with the severe taping and the restrictions it created, I had to become a slasher. And consequently, I think I got punished a lot more."

In other words, Roger had to stop running like Curt Warner and start running like John Cappelletti.

"You're absolutely correct," Kochman admitted. "And I never had John Cappelletti's size or strength. And I think Curt Warner has much more mobility than I would have even without the restriction. But the interesting thing about that cartilage injury was that a guy who showed up at the Bills' training camp was just one of the group. I was one of the few who had only one damaged knee. And, before I got hurt in the regular season, I had no injuries. That was the first time playing football, except for the normal bumps and bruises, that I can remember playing in pain. I didn't practice in pain. I really think I was getting back to having fun playing football.

"I didn't even make the traveling squad for the first two regular-season games. They had tried me at wide receiver in the pre-season, and I hadn't gotten much playing time at running back. But what happened was they lost a couple of running backs when they were away. Ray Carlton got hurt early, and Glenn Bass. So I was thrust back to running back. I got very limited playing time in the third game, but I think I started the fourth and had a good game. So I started the fifth, sixth and seventh games. My first start at War Memorial Coliseum, I gained something like 98 yards and caught a couple of passes for good gains. In the sixth game against Kansas City, I scored my only pro touchdown on a pass and I think I ran for 88 yards in that game. And then I got hurt."

Hurt is putting it mildly. Twenty years later, people wince when Kochman talks about the play that ended his football career and almost ended his ambulatory life.

"We were at Houston and we had a third-and-one situation and I got called to carry the ball," he said. "It was a trap play inside. I got the handoff and got hit behind the line by a guy by the name of Dudley Meridith, who weighed about 300 pounds. I had him draped over my shoulder, but I figured I had third-and-one so I'd try to carry him for the yard. I attempted to pivot and my foot locked in the ground. My body was totally turned around, my foot was locked and, at that point, I got hit from the side by Houston's defensive end, a kid named Gary Cutsinger. Essentially, I almost tore the leg off. The only thing that wasn't severed was the skin. Everything internally, including the artery, was severed. The thing I think I remember most was lying on the ground and looking at the bottom of my foot. It was an incredible experience.

"The fortunate thing, if there was anything fortunate about the whole experience, is that the game was in Houston. I ended up going to Methodist Hospital and was attended not only by some good orthopedic surgeons but the arterial damage that I suffered was supervised by Michael DeBakey, who just happened to be in the hospital the night I went in for emergency surgery. And they did a lot of work to save my leg.

"The artery became the critical item. It was such a clean separation that it didn't show up initially on x-rays. So after they had reset my leg, hours later, the artery physically separated and I began to collect blood in my lower leg. As a result of that whole thing, I suffered permanent nerve damage, permanent circulatory damage, and lost half of my foot. All the toes and about half my foot.

"I've coped with it fairly well, I think. It has been kind of an interesting experience that has buttressed my belief in the power of the human mind. Initially I was in a drop-foot control brace for three years because I had no control of my foot. I couldn't pick my foot up to do normal walking. Once I got out of the drop-foot control brace, I got as far as playing squash and racquetball. I took up golf about 10 years ago and I enjoy that. The hardest thing is getting used to living with pain. I've had constant pain since the injury. Some days are better than others. For years after the accident, I was on a regular dose of medication to control the pain. But finally I decided it was senseless to go through the rest of my life with narcotics. That can't have any good permanent effect. So at this point in time, when the pain gets extremely bad, I'll take aspirin or something like that.

"I try not to think about what will happen when I'm 50 or 55. It's not worth contemplating what may happen."

And, hard as it may be to believe, Roger Kochman can never remember being turned off—or turning off—a game of football since the awful injury.

"It's never really bothered me," he said. "I think the only thing that bothers me now in watching football games is some of the cheap shots. Cheap shots are not part of the game and people who have to resort to that tactic I don't think should be in the game. Violence is part of the game, but you have to control that violence. It's like anything else. Anyone who loses personal control over themselves, it's a problem. And it's especially true with the size of the football players today. That body is almost a weapon out there.

"You talk about different experiences in football. High school football, maybe you have three good kids on the team. Get to college and maybe 75 percent of the kids on the team have equal kinds of talent. And then you get up to the pros and you just don't separate them. The higher you go in football, physical attributes don't dominate. Motivation takes over. People who want to play end up playing.

"I had some doubts quite honestly about whether or not I had the ability to play pro football. But I think once I got exposed to it and figured out that I could play it, I had just gotten back to my old self."

And just as suddenly, a cruel accident told him that he would never play it again. So he went back to Penn State and got his master's degree and went to work for the telephone company. First in Pittsburgh, then he was transferred to Philadelphia in the midst of a big corporate reorganization.

"My title now is district staff manager in charge of quality of work life," he said. "Our company has decided that we would like to develop a more participatory style of management, to allow all of our employees the chance to have a say in those decisions which not only affect how they work but the conditions under which they work. So I'm essentially a staff of one for both Pennsylvania and Delaware with the responsibility of incorporating that style of management into our ongoing activities. I deal not only with our managers but with all five of our unions, seeing that the process filters down and is maintained throughout our organization. I was put into this position in November, 1981. Before that, I was in labor relations. But I spent most of my career in the operations end of the business."

Kochman's personal life was undergoing a change at the time of this interview. He and his wife had been separated for three years and had instituted divorce proceedings. Through the separation, though, he had maintained close contact with his daughter Stacey, twelve, and son Douglas, eight. Both children's pictures are on display in his office behind his desk. And if Douglas suddenly said one weekend that he wanted to play football?

"I guess I would approach it in this respect," he answered. "Whatever my kids want to do, whatever my son wants to do, I will help him. I will encourage him. I would not push him toward football, nor would I push him toward anything else. And I wouldn't push him away from it. That's a decision I think he has to make.

"I've had good experiences out of football and I've had bad experiences. I think it's just part of life. The same thing could have happened to someone walking off a curb, getting hit by a car, whatever. You can't anticipate it. It's an accident. I would not overly encourage him (to play football) unless it was his decision that he really wanted to do it. Then I would help him to do it as best as he possibly could."

In the meantime, he copes with it all—a broken marriage, commuter trains, life at the phone company, a golf game that occasionally dips into the 70's, and the constant reminder in his right leg of football's legacy to him.

"I think I was lucky," he says now, "in going beyond the initial feeling of being sorry for myself when I got hurt, the 'Hey, what did I do to deserve this?' to the 'Hey, you don't really have a choice right now. Your life is going to be what you make it. No one's going to do anything else for you.'

"I like to think I've made the best of it."

Chuck Burkhart gets set to pass.

2
CHUCK BURKHART

People will always look at an athlete like Roger Kochman and think in terms of what might have been. They will remember the bumps and bruises that plagued his career at Penn State and the baseball injury that turned him from speedster to slasher. And they will note the pro career that ended after five games, four starts, 232 rushing yards, four pass receptions and one touchdown and wonder what kind of stats he might have amassed in a full career.

Chuck Burkhart is the other side of the coin—a quarterback whose career never reached the pro level, yet could easily be characterized as one of overachievement. In the two years he started for Joe Paterno, he was often compared with his coach in terms of playing career. Invariably, a quote from the late Stanley Woodward, written in 1949 when Paterno was Rip Engle's quarterback at Brown, surfaced. "He can't run and he can't pass," Woodward wrote of Paterno. "All he can do is think—and win!" And everyone would guffaw a bit and say, sure, isn't it amazing how Paterno picked a quarterback in his own football image and likeness. Had Burkhart come along a decade later, he would have been known as Paterno's Clone.

In reality, the comparisons are very unfair—to Burkhart, that is. Consider this: As a player at Brooklyn Prep and Brown, Paterno won most of his games. As the starting quarterback at Montour High School in McKees Rocks, Pa., and at Penn State, Chuck Burkhart won **all** his games. Included were back-to-back Orange Bowls. And, if they didn't talk national championship at University Park in Roger Kochman's days, the topic had become bitter enough to involve the President of the United States by the time Burkhart had thrown his final collegiate pass.

Burkhart was the Rodney Dangerfield of college football. He didn't get no respect. Ethnic jokes were sweeping the country and there was even a Chuck Burkhart joke. It went like this: On first down, Burkhart underthrew his receiver. On second down, he overthrew him. On third down, he was intercepted. He was so angry at himself when he got to the sideline that he took off his helmet and disgustedly threw it at the ground—and missed.

Maybe what they forget is that Burkhart threw the pass that resulted in the only touchdown of the 1970 Orange Bowl. He didn't miss Lydell Mitchell with that little pop to the left flat. And he threw the most famous pass in Penn State history—the 47-yard desperation heave to Bobby Campbell that helped turn defeat to victory in the 1969 Orange Bowl. And maybe they also forget that he completed over half his passes (146-for-291) for 1,975 games as a starter in those two back-to-back unbeaten regular seasons.

"If you have to have impressive statistics to be great," Paterno said of Burkhart between Chuck's junior and senior seasons, "he's never going to be great. But if you base his value on how many games he wins for you and will win for you he's great. All I know is that as quarterback in two years of high school, his teams were 20-0. Last'year, we were 11-0. That's 31-0 and you can't beat that without cheating."

His career would up 42-0 and you can't beat that even if you do cheat!

So why was Chuck Burkhart Rodney Dangerfield's favorite quarterback? Part of it had to be that Burkhart simply didn't look like a football player, at least not a player for an undefeated major college team that played in back-to-back major bowl games. If Paterno had his Stanley Woodward, Burkhart had his Roy McHugh. The **Pitts-Press** columnist pointed out that the two most prominent features of Burkhart were his horn-rimmed glasses and an omnipresent smile, "both of which he removes only to play football."

In fact, you might say that Chuck Burkhart's present job fits his image more than someone barking signals on third-and-four. Chuck Burkhart is a Pepper. As in, "Wouldn't you like to be a Pepper, too? Be a Pepper, drink Dr. Pepper." He works out of the main office of the company in Dallas, where he is a region sales manager, one of four. His territory? "Eastern part of Texas, over to the Carolinas and everything south of there," he says.

And how many of you immediately thought, "If he had to cover that territory with completed passes, nobody in the South would be drinking anything but Coke or Pepsi?" Sometime you get nailed with a label and it sticks for life. And what about the no-pass label? Does it still bother him? Did it ever bother him?

"I think it bothered me at the time because of getting picked at for what you thought was a pretty decent job," he said. "Plus, I think we did a lot of things right. Like I always tell people, if we had had someone who was better, he would have played."

**Chuck Burkhart threw one of the most famous passes in Penn State history—
the 47-yard desperation heave to Bobby Campbell that helped turn defeat to
victory in the 1969 Orange Bowl.**

Right there, Chuck might have hit on the real reason why he got no respect. He was looked upon as the most visible potential weak link on a team which in reality had none. The defense got all the headlines—Mike Reid and Steve Smear and Jim Kates and Jack Ham and Dennis Onkotz and Neal Smith were the big names. Four of the running backs—Bobby Campbell, Charlie Pittman, Franco Harris and Lydell Mitchell—have had pro careers of varying degrees of success. The tight end on the 1968 Orange Bowl squad, Ted Kwalick, had already been praised by Paterno as "the greatest tight end I've ever seen." He later had a long and successful pro career. The quarterback the year before Burkhart started, Tom Sherman, played in the pros. The quarterback the year after he started, John Hufnagel, made the pros. The man who snapped him the ball, Warren Koegel, played professional football, for goodness sake. So there it was. Everybody around him was a potential pro, Burkhart was not. Ergo, the weak link theory.

And even Chuck himself will poke some fun at his former teammates, knowing they would give it back to him. There was an extremely important play in the fourth game of the 1968 season at the Los Angeles Coliseum. It

Joe Paterno gives instructions to quarterback Chuck Burkhart during game at Beaver Stadium.

was a game the Lions were to win, 21-6, and a victory that made the nation sit up and notice this team from Central Pennsylvania. In the third quarter, Penn State was sitting on a 7-0 lead and had the ball at its 24. Burkhart rolled out, then suddenly spun and threw the ball in the opposite direction to Tom Cherry, a fullback who did not list speed on his football resume.

"It's a play Penn State always runs," Burkhart recalled. "Tom went 76 yards and he didn't get 76 yards the rest of the year. What we did was flood the zones and hope to read the weakness of the defense. Usually there is someone out there and it becomes a one-on-one thing. But on that play, they blitzed, so Tom was out there all alone. I got him the ball, and 10 minutes later he crossed the goal line. He might be able to make fun of my arm, but I can make fun of his legs."

That play helped set up the unbeaten season and the bid to the Orange Bowl, the Nittany Lions' first major post-season trip in 21 years. And, after what happened in the last 76 seconds of the game with Kansas in Miami, people briefly stopped making fun of Chuck Burkhart's arm. And no one ever questioned his leadership or will to win.

"It's still a great thought," says Burkhart of the incredible finish. "It's a great memory, one that comes up on more than one occasion. There's a great sense of satisfaction in being able to look back and tell yourself, 'Yeah, I did score a touchdown and, yeah, I did throw a pass and we were able to pull a game out of the fire.' And for me, there was recognition, which I had not received much of before. Rather than being someone who sort of cemented a lot of great athletes together, now there was a series of plays that I could look back to in which I was able to do something to help toward a victory."

The first thing Burkhart was able to do was complete a seemingly impossible pass with a minute and a half left and the ball at midfield in a game the Kansas Jayhawks seemingly had under perfect control. People who saw it rubbed their eyes in disbelief. And the passer himself saw it for the first time on film.

"Actually the play we called we had never tried before," Burkhart said. "We had not been a long-pass, home-run type offense. I don't think any Penn State team has ever been. But this was a case of looking at the situation and asking ourselves what we were going to do. And we decided that (the long pass) was going to be it.

"The one thing that's hard to express in words is the feeling of those Penn State teams when I was there. You never really thought about losing. You just never did. A lot of it had to do with the players who were there and the great job the coaches did. I don't think in any sporting event I ever thought about losing. Sometime you lose and sometime you win, but we were there at a very fortunate and right time for a lot a great young people.

"It was a multi-personality team. Mike Reid was a lot different than I was. You had Ted Kwalick. You had Denny Onkotz. You had Pete Johnson. You had a lot of what I would classify as not only very good athletes, but also smart people. And the one thing that we did have in common was that nobody ever thought about losing. Now here was a play we had never tried before and everyone knows that when you have a long passing team, the thing that makes it work is timing. We didn't have any timing on the play. One of our guys, I don't know who it was, missed a block and I've got this Kansas guy barrelling down on me and I don't even see Bobby Campbell. I'm back and I get the pass off and it's either going to be complete or it's going to be over someone's head. Or short. Or whatever. I knew I had thrown a good pass because you can always feel that. But on the other hand, they've got a prevent defense working on Bobby, who doesn't exactly run a 4.4 40.

"And now one of their guys tries to intercept the ball. Who in the stadium would have figured that? Maybe if he had just gone up with Bobby I would have knocked the ball away. Who knows? But Bobby makes a great catch and runs it down to the three yard line. And me? I have no idea what's going on because I'm eating grass. I heard a roar and I knew something had happened but I didn't know if it was good for us or them."

But the drama was just starting with that play. Two times Cherry tried to plunge off tackle. The total yield: Zero yards. The Nittany Lions were still three yards and eight points short on third down. Paterno sent in a different play.

"The call was for a scissors," Burkhart said. "We had been running off left tackle for two plays with Tom Cherry. We still had three yards to pick up for the score. So the next play in that series would be a fake to the fullback and then give it to the slotback on a reverse. That was the play Joe had called.

"It's a play that is either going to totally fool everybody or go nowhere. And what happened was that a very aggressive Kansas defense was able to get into the ball-handling of the play. Through the coaching that I had—and it was done instinctively—I kept the ball and went to the left and made it to the end zone.

"Nobody on our team was about to think that it was either score the touchdown or it would be the offense's last play of the game, so we were able to startle the defense and go in for the score."

The startled defense for the Jayhawks had been your basic 5-3-4 because an extra linebacker had entered the game after Burkhart hit Campbell with the pass no one left the field. And—until the extra-points try—no one had noticed.

Burkhart dropped back and threw an incomplete pass to Kwalick and the Kansas fans went wild. But the umpire, Foster Grose, had finally noticed that there were too many Jayhawks on the field and threw his flag. But even as the pass to Kwalick was dropped incomplete, Burkhart was still thinking victory.

"You're harried because they do have 12 men on the field and the one defensive end (Vernon Vanoy), he's 6-8 and he's on your back and you think, 'Hey, I've got to throw the ball. I've got nothing else I can do.' The ball

Chuck Burkhart . . . today.

is incomplete and you see a flag right away. You figure, 'He's not going to throw this flag if it's against me,' and instead you immediately think, 'What's happening, what's next?' And when you get the call, you've got a chance from even closer. And so there never was a down feeling within myself because there never was any time to absorb it. It's difficult to go from the high we were experiencing from completing the long pass, from scoring the touchdown. Ten seconds later, here you are with another shot at the win. We were still pumped up at the time from the pass and from the score. There was not enough time for Kansas to get picked up and not enough time for us to get down. Really, I don't think there was a doubt in anybody's mind that we would score. Heck, we all thought we were going to score on the pass."

Now the call was for a run off left tackle by Campbell. Offensive guard Charlie Zapiec pulled and blocked John Zook. Fullback Cherry blocked linebacker Emery Hicks. Campbell slipped slightly wide of tackle and dove into the end zone. And after the kickoff and one weary pass to nowhere by Bobby Douglass, the Nittany Lions had polished off one of the most dramatic bowl victories of all time.

"The play was designed to gain a yard and people never give Campbell the proper amount of credit," said Burkhart about the game-winner. "He was just a great back, especially a clutch back. You couldn't ask for a better guy to give the ball at the time. Of course, if Franco Harris had been a year older, I know who would have gotten the ball."

The following autumn, the Nittany Lions marched through their regular season, threatened only by Syracuse which went under by a point, thanks to a fourth quarter rally. While some people might remember it as merely a continuation of the 1968 season, Burkhart remembers it as a year of transition.

"We had graduated so many exceptional offensive players from that first Orange Bowl team," he said. "Ted Kwalick would do so many things for our offense. And who did we replace him with? Pete Johnson, who was an exceptional athlete but who had been a linebacker all the time at State. And you don't move someone from linebacker to tight end and expect to execute a tight-end-oriented offense. Greg Edmonds was the split end, but in our ball-control offense, all you threw him were outs and curls. And Greg was no 4.3 speedster, either, and that was a good thing because I probably never would have gotten the ball to him. And we lost two great blockers in Dave Bradley and John Kulka. At running back, you replace Bobby Campbell and Tom Cherry with Franco Harris and Lydell Mitchell. The change you have there is in experience. There was no doubt about their abilities. They were unbelievable, they were great—but they were also green.

"In both those years, I think the word for our team was cohesive. I don't ever remember any arguments, any fights. Guys screwed around at times, but it was always healthy. There was no moodiness, just a bunch of good people who stayed together before and after the season as well as during the season.

"I just think that was the kind of athlete Penn State was getting. You never had to worry about the school or the team being embarrassed. In fact, on the contrary. The athletes usually added something to everything."

That particular year the football players added a second Orange Bowl trophy to the athletic department's showcase. Also that particular year, Richard Nixon added some spice to the season by declaring before the Texas-Arkansas game that the winner would be national champion and that he would be there to present the plaque. No one was quite sure who had designated the President as the sole selector of the national championship, especially a bespectacled young head coach in State College, Pa. Paterno screamed long and loud that his team had every right to be in the running for the national title. But Nixon's Southern strategy had spread to the gridiron. He announced that he would present Penn State with a plaque honoring the football team's win streak, longest in the nation. Paterno told the President what he could do with his plaque, and he wasn't going to put it in the Rec Hall trophy case.

And the Nittany Lions opted to go to the Orange Bowl to play Missouri instead of the Cotton Bowl to play either Texas or Arkansas.

"A lot of people forget the circumstance," Burkhart said. "We had been second the year before. And now, at the time when we were voting where we wanted to go, we were ranked third, behind Ohio State and Texas. If hindsight is right, sure, we would have come to Dallas to play for number one. But what was the sense of going to Dallas to see who was number two when you had already been number two the year before?

"Besides, the Orange Bowl had treated us so royally the year before. And here we are, a bunch of kids from Pennsylvania, Ohio, New York and New Jersey. When you're from those states and you think about where you want to go in the wintertime, the answer isn't Dallas, Texas. It's Florida. So, for anyone in that position, it was a simple discussion. And to us, the Orange Bowl was even a more glamorous game because it was at night. The whole country had to either watch you or be asleep with a hangover."

And the hangover remains for Burkhart and his teammates. Richard Nixon, the national pollsters and the state of Texas aside, the Nittany Lions had their own ideas about the national championship. Missouri coach Dan Devine got on the bandwagon after the 10-3 loss in Miami. "I don't know if Penn State could have scored on the Texas defense," he said, "but I do know one thing. Texas never would have scored on the Penn State defense."

"I think my senior year that Penn State was the best team in the country," Burkhart said. "And my junior year, if we had had the opportunity to play someone? You just never know.

"The only team that was going to give that second Orange Bowl team any trouble was a team that could run the ball and pass the ball very well. And neither of those teams in the Cotton Bowl were going to do that. In fact, Notre Dame might have given us more trouble than Texas. Paterno was always way ahead of his peers defensively. Offensively was another story, but I'm sure his strategy was, 'Hey, if they don't score, we don't lose.' And it's kind of tough to find fault with that. It just seemed that we were always capable of doing whatever we had to do to win.

"It seemed to me that Penn State always recruited with the idea of putting the most talented players on defense. The exceptions might have been running backs like Mitchell and Harris, plus Pittman who was a great running back.

"We were a true small-town environment at State College. I would always classify Penn Staters as being a tad naive compared to the students from the big city colleges. At some of the other places, you always heard about kids worrying that someone was getting more than someone else. At Penn State, nobody even worried about making All-American. Nobody worried about the pro contracts. And it made it a helluva lot nicer."

In many ways, Burkhart is Paterno's Clone as far as post-collegiate careers go, too. Paterno was on his way to law school and decided to help Rip Engle for just one season at Penn State. He never left. On the other hand, Burkhart spent his college career planning to teach and coach. He decided to try the business world "for a year or so." And he has stayed in it, starting right out of college with Proctor and Gamble before switching to Dr. Pepper last year. But he says he would have taken a chance at coaching if his high school head coach and Penn State assistant Bob Phillips had gotten a chance at a top college job.

"When I student-taught, I saw some things that made me think I might be better off going into the business world and using my God-given talents to lead in selling situations," he said. "A lot of it was the fact that they were willing to pay a lot more money at the time in business. So I figured I would give it my best shot and, if it didn't work out, I could go into teaching and coaching.

"Quite honestly, if Bob Phillips had been given the opportunity to be a head coach, be it at Penn State or Pitt or wherever, and if he had wanted me on his staff, that's probably what I would be doing today. Beside my father, there's no one who has done more to help me than Bob Phillips. And I don't just mean athletically. He was always there to count on. You could talk with him and he didn't talk down to you. But when he was coaching and he said, you had to do it this way, you did it this way, especially in high school.

"That's probably where I started getting the winning attitude, at Montour High, because we never lost. It's a unique thing to spend a career in football and only being able to remember one game in which you got your nose bloodied. That was the Big 33 game. Coach Phillips always encouraged you. He taught you to be as good as you could be and that after that there's nothing else you can do. And he's right. That's why I had always wished he would get the opportunity to be a head coach in college."

Bob Phillips is still an assistant to Paterno at Penn State and Burkhart is in Dallas—the city he and his teammates shunned in 1969—selling the Penn State of soft drinks. It's not going to be easy for Dr. Pepper to get to be number one, either, but Burkhart is trying to lead it in that direction.

He and his wife Grace and his three sons, who are between the ages of five and twelve, have found happiness in Texas. And, while his Orange Bowl heroics changed the course of Penn State football history, they have never changed his sense of perspective.

"There have been so many more occasions that have been so much more important to my life since then," he said. "Getting married, the birth of my children. The experiences of growing up with your children, the experiences you share with your wife, I believe that they become much more important than other things you can reach back for, much more than scoring a touchdown, even though that was the pinnacle of my athletic career."

Chuck Burkhart's Clone, the man who leads the Penn State football team, would agree wholeheartedly.

John Cappelletti, who gained 2,639 yards in his career, ranks as the third highest rusher in Penn State history.

3

JOHN CAPPELLETTI

I f Chuck Burkhart captured the imagination of America with his desperation pass to Bobby Campbell in the 1969 Orange Bowl, John Cappelletti stole the nation's heart in a Manhattan hotel ballroom five Decembers later.

People who were there will never forget it. By the time Cappelletti was finished speaking, eight thousand wet eyes filled the room. All the networks showed the film clips the next evening, and people across the country were able to share in the most poignant acceptance speech in the history of the Heisman Trophy.

A movie made for television about the special relationships between cancer-stricken Brian Piccolo and Gale Sayers had made the country cry a few years earlier. A movie made for television about the special relationship between John and Joey Cappelletti would make the nation weep a few years later. But nothing will ever compare with the real thing at the New York Hilton on that December night in 1973.

The evening started out poorly. One of the Downtown Athletic Club stuffed-shirt types told an unfunny joke that centered around physical afflictions and need not be repeated. The keynote speaker was then Vice President Gerald Ford, which explained all those men in business suits with buttons in their ears swarming around the area. And very quickly we learned that the Vice President hadn't done his homework. He congratulated "Joe Cappelletti" and referred to "my good friend, Coach John Fraterno." But the quiet murmuring that always underscores a packed banquet hall quickly died as John Cappelletti began his acceptance speech.

After missing all but three plays of Syracuse game, John Cappelletti came back strong against West Virginia on his way to the 1973 Heisman Trophy.

"There were a lot of feelings that night," Cappelletti reminisced almost nine years later from his home in Orange County's Westminster, Cal., 25 miles south of Los Angeles. "Number one, I was just feeling good inside because of what had happened to me and how it was affecting so many people. Not just my family and friends but the university and the people I had played with. I realized all the coaches were in New York at the time. It was just a case of a lot of people being involved in something that had never happened at Penn State before. I think if it had happened before, it wouldn't have been the same feeling for me. Now it may not be on the same level, but I think they'll get the same feeling back at Penn State when they win the national championship. That's never been achieved either, and the first time is always a little nicer because it evokes kind of a sigh of relief within all the excitement. It's over with, it happened and nobody can take it away from you —that kind of feeling.

"The speech itself was basically an extension of mostly thanking people who had contributed to my development throughout the different stages of my life, up to that point..."

A week ago, or ten days ago, when the Heisman Trophy was announced, I hadn't had too much time to think about what it has meant. I think listening to former Heisman Trophy winners tonight and seeing everyone here to share in it and congratulate me on it is one of the first steps I have taken in the meaning of this trophy. I'm sure that the people behind me know much more about it than I do, and I'm happy for any advice they have given tonight on what to expect from the future with this trophy.

I have had time to think about some of the things that have put me up here tonight, things that have happened in my life and I'd like to reflect on them now.

I think the first thing that happened was that God blessed me with a great deal of talent and a lot of people to complement that talent. My family as everyone has met, mostly I guess, are great people and I'm very happy to have shared in my lifetime with them. My brothers and sisters have been wonderful. Just being with them the past few years, they have always been behind me and I can't express that enough. My mother and father—there isn't a greater couple around. I know my mother always cries at these affairs, so I want to try not to. She's a very, very strong woman and dedicated, not only to her children and husband, but also to God and I think this helped her out with putting up with us and going through all she has gone through. I think one small example of this, a personal thing with me that I think a lot of people may have noticed, is that my legs are as straight as arrows and that I have no trouble walking now, or running, but one time in my life I couldn't walk without tripping. My mother not only brought me through this, but she brought just about every member of our family through something like this.

My father is a very quiet man; he's been a great father to all of us. He asked me the other day when I was home what I thought of him as a father. I wouldn't say much to him then because it's hard to express things like that, but there is no greater person I have more respect for than this man.

I think the next event that was most important to me in my life was when I went to high school and I was fortunate enough to be coached by a man who dedicated himself, not only to his players on the field but very much so off the field. He's a great lover of football. He'd sacrifice anything for a teammate or a player when he was playing and when he was coaching. He passed away this summer, Jack Gottshalk, but I think in the 43 years he was here on earth, he did more for young people and people he was associated with than most of us get a chance to do in our lifetime.

The next step I think, was going to Penn State. It was a hard decision making a choice of colleges. At the time, I didn't know much about it, but I think the one thing that swayed me was the man sitting to my right, and that is coach Paterno. When I was being recruited, he came down to my house. I think he was not only on a recruiting trip, but he was looking for a good meal, an Italian meal. When he came in the door, he looked over, and on the couch was my brother, Joseph, lying there. He was very ill at the time, more so than usual, and instead of—that is not a joke —coach Paterno was more concerned and talked more about what he could do for my brother than what he could do to get me at Penn State. For this, I am very thankful and I'm glad I had the chance to show some appreciation to this man in the past four years. I think everyone here knows mostly about his coaching accomplishments at Penn State. His record is a great one, probably the greatest in the country. He has carried on a great tradition at Penn State, I think, which started with Rip Engle. He's more concerned with young people after they get out of school than when they are in school - what he can do for them to make better lives for them not only on the football field, but in life itself.

I think Vice President Ford said, "You can't compare life to a football game but you can compare a football game to life" and I think this is what he (Paterno) has tried to show us in my four years there and in the years he has been coaching and teaching. I don't think there is a more dedicated man anywhere concerned with young people and a better teacher of life on and off the field.

The next group of people I'm going to talk about, I've been with for four years and I've played with them. They are my teammates this year, the seniors and the co-captains whom you have met down here. I don't think I've ever been closer to a group of people who I've worked with, sweated with, and done more with in four years than with anybody else in my lifetime. I don't think I could have gotten any closer to the group that I have been with and I think that it takes a lot of hard work to do what we've done this year. I'm just glad I did my part for my teammates and that we've had the season we've had, the closeness that we've had, and for them I'm thankful just for that.

Also, there is a coach here tonight who I am very proud of. He's our backfield coach at Penn State. His name is Bob Phillips. I think he's mainly responsible for a lot of the attitude that goes on at Penn State among the players. He's a very dedicated man to his work, but he goes about it with a healthy and bright attitude. He relays this to the players to the point where you want to do things for him and you take the attitude that you are not out there just to get finished and go in and take a shower, but you are out there to accomplish something. People like him are the reason that I think a lot of the players, and I know myself, were out there this year doing the things we did, and I'd like to thank him for that.

The next part—I'm very happy to do something like this—I thought about it since the Heisman was announced ten days ago, and this is to dedicate a trophy that a lot of people earned, I've earned, my parents and all the people I've mentioned and numerous other people that are here tonight and (have) been with me for a long time.

John Cappelletti had delivered it all with a quivering voice that seemed ready to collapse. And now it finally did.

"The part with Joey was difficult, but I just felt that way about him," John recalled. "In fact, I probably felt a little closer to him, and more on a level that you don't really have to talk about. But it seemed like that was the time to do it."

The youngest member of my family, Joseph, is very ill. He has leukemia. If I can dedicate this trophy to him tonight and give him a couple days of happiness, this is worth everything. I think a lot of people think that I go through a lot on Saturdays and during the week as most athletes do, and you get your bumps and bruises and it is a terrific battle out there on the field. Only for me it is on Saturdays and it's only in the Fall. For Joseph it is all year round and it is a battle that is unending with him and he puts up with much more than I'll ever put up with and I think that this trophy is more his than mine because he has been a great inspiration to me.

I'd just like to thank everyone here tonight for putting up with me, the Downtown Athletic Club for having this affair and the way they've treated myself, my parents and the guests from Penn State these last few days. I don't think I'll ever forget this night. Thank you.

The applause from the jammed room was long and sincere, and then it was time for the benediction. The late Archbishop Fulton J. Sheen, who was a great speaker, a man who had attracted tremendous television audiences for his show in the 1950's, got the call. And this time he gave one of his most memorable speeches—short, punchy, to the point.

"Maybe for the first time in your lives, you have heard a speech from the heart and not from the lips," Sheen said. "Part of John's triumph was made by Joseph's sorrow. You don't need a blessing. God has already blessed you in John Cappelletti."

At the table in front of the dias, Joey Cappelletti was beaming. John had indeed given his brother the first of several days of happiness before his death on April 8, 1976. The 11-year-old would battle back from his illness enough to be able to play some organized Little League baseball. He would make several more trips up to Lion Country to watch another brother, Michael, play for the Nittany Lions. And he could often be seen in the post-game locker room, walking from dressing stall to dressing stall, talking to some of the players.

At those moments, it was as if John Cappelletti had never left the campus for professional football.

"I don't know how to put this," John explained, "but going on those Penn State trips was something Joey enjoyed because of all the good things that were in it for him. The atmosphere surrounding it. Knowing players. Even at that point in his life he was much more aware of what went on in the sports world than I had been. I mean, he could actually tell you who Joe Paterno was, or who certain players on the team were and what it meant to be playing college football, whereas when I was that age, if my parents had brought me up to Penn State, I wouldn't have had any idea about what was going on. But he really identified with it that way.

"His was the kind of life where he enjoyed it when he could, when he was basically healthy. And I think that was the real release for him up at Penn State, to be healthy and to be able to participate in that kind of atmosphere. It was almost a representation of him feeling good and being healthy. Maybe he associated that with Penn State. And he had a relationship with some of the guys on that team that a lot of young people never have the opportunity to have. Maybe it was meant to happen that way because he wasn't going to be around as long as most of us.

John Cappelletti and former President Gerald Ford on a very special night in New York City in December, 1973.

"I do know this. After being up there for a couple of years, he was in his second term. He was becoming a professional student."

By that time, John Cappelletti had become the consummate professional athlete. Other guys carried the ball more often or scored more touchdowns but if a crisp block from the upback was needed to break off the long gain, Cappelletti supplied it.

It was kind of the style that had carried him from Monsignor Bonner to Penn State. When he was recruited from the suburban Philadelphia high school, no one made a big deal out of it. Penn State didn't like to publicize its recruits anyway, but when a fellow Delaware County prospect named Steve Joachim announced for Penn State, the Philadelphia papers trumpeted the news with banner headlines. John Cappelletti's decision was announced in the middle of the notes in the schoolboy writers' columns.

Which was about the way things should have been. Joachim, you see, had already been proclaimed "The Quarterback of the Seventies" by **Sport Magazine**. Virtually every college in the country wanted his signature. Beside setting national passing records (one of his receivers was Steeler tight end Randy Grossman), Joachim was bright and glib. He had size and an arm with the distance that would make many a pro quarterback blush.

Cappelletti was also a quarterback in high school, so his achievements at Bonner were dwarfed by Joachim's feats at nearby Haverford High. The biggest reason was that Cappy was strictly a running quarterback (Bonner's passing attack was practically nil).

After a season at tailback in which he led the freshman team in running, John received a surprise during pre-season drills. He had worked as the number-two tailback during the previous spring, but Paterno called him in one late summer day and proposed a one-season switch, to defensive back.

"There wasn't too much of a reaction within myself," Cappelletti recalls. "I just wanted to make sure I would be moved back. And, basically, that was the agreement. I realized I wasn't going to be playing much on offense (behind senior record-setter Lydell Mitchell).

"Joe had me returning punts and kickoffs, which wasn't the best move he ever made. He put me in kind of an awkward position of trying to become a defensive back in a year's time. That's not done very effectively unless you are just a naturally good defensive player."

Which Cappelletti was not. His legs were too muscular. Besides that, it was extremely difficult for a man who spent his entire career up to then running forward to suddenly find himself trying to learn to backpedal against a wide receiver with 4.5 speed.

"If he had wanted to put me at linebacker, it probably would have been better," Cappy said. "But I guess he needed defensive backs badly. At one point, the three defensive backs in the lineup were myself, Eddie O'Neil and

Greg Ducatte. It wasn't one of the best defensive backfields in history, but it had to be one of the biggest. Eddie and I used to bring back punts and it was like a circus back there once in a while when we would run into each other. But I was able to live with that season. I figured it would be better doing something rather than nothing at all."

Nothing at all is what Cappelletti did the following season in the Sugar Bowl after helping Penn State trounce Texas, 30-6, in the Cotton Bowl his sophomore year. The transition from defense back to offense was exactly what Cappelletti needed. During the regular season, he scored 13 touchdowns, rushed for 1,117 yards and a 4.8 average and did a lot to fill the spot vacated by Mitchell. Penn State lost its opener at Tennessee, then won ten straight. Its Sugar Bowl opponent was Oklahoma, which Paterno publicly said was the best team his squad would have faced in half a dozen years. Privately, though, Paterno felt he could beat the Sooners with a ball-control offense featuring his punishing tailback.

But Joe's plans went, excuse the expression, down the drain on the eve of the game at Tulane Stadium. Cappelletti woke up well past midnight and realized when he was having trouble making it to the bathroom under his own power that there would be no making it to the line of scrimmage the following evening.

"Everything had gone so well during that week," Cappy remembered, "but the night before the game, in the middle of the night, I woke up sick. I couldn't keep anything down. I just became very miserable, felt very bad. There wasn't much I could do at that point except letting the people in charge know and letting the doctors know. There was no way I was capable of playing a game at that point.

"It was a bad situation because Walt Addie, who was the second tailback, had missed much of the practice that week because of a bad ankle. If he had been able to get the practice time, he would have been more comfortable and been more accustomed to the offense. But there wasn't much I could do about anything. Even at game time, I only saw a little bit of the transmission of the game, I was in such bad shape."

Without Cappelletti, the Nittany Lion running attack had the power of a marshmallow. Addie was ineffective on his gimpy ankle, fullback Bob Nagle was only able to gain 22 yards in 10 carries; Penn State finished the night with 49 rushing yards and a 14-0 defeat.

There would be one more absolutely miserable day in Cappelletti's college career as a senior—at Syracuse. He had come up with a shoulder injury that ruled out any contact. Paterno used him on the first series as a decoy. Three times Tom Shuman took the ball and handed off to the other backs. Syracuse was not fooled. Cappy went to the bench for the rest of the game.

Addie was also on the shelf with a blood disorder, so Paterno called on sophomore Woody Petchel, who had led the state of Pennsylvania in scoring two seasons back. Woody went down with a severely torn knee that ended his season and Paterno was down to his fourth tailback, a heretofore answer to a trivia question named Rusty Boyle. No matter. Penn State won, 49-6, and people wondered if the lack of stats against the Orangemen would hurt Cappelletti in the Heisman balloting.

Penn State, meanwhile, didn't exactly know what to do about the Heisman question. In the early 1950's, Lenny Moore was the match for any running back in the country but the school didn't try to push him until after the season. Then, in 1959, now-athletic director Jim Tarman made a big pre-season publicity push for All-America on behalf of quarterback Richie Lucas —and almost sneaked away with the Heisman as a bonus. Lucas finished second to LSU's Billy Cannon. In 1971, the dilemma was twofold. Lydell Mitchell and Franco Harris were both seniors. And, in the early season, it was hard to pick a candidate between them. Lydell scored five TD's in the opener against Navy and gained 211 yards in 29 carries in the second game against Iowa. But in the Iowa game, Harris gained 145 yards on 28 cracks and scored four TD's. So Penn State packaged the duo as Mr. Inside and Mr. Outside. That was terrific except that Mr. Inside (Mitchell) wound up scoring 29 touchdowns and gaining over 1,500 yards while Mr. Outside (Harris) settled for 687 rushing yards and seven scores. Mr. Inside finished fifth in the Heisman voting, which was won by Auburn quarterback Pat Sullivan, who went on to perform a disappearing act in the pros.

That lesson having been learned, Penn State in 1972 mounted a campaign for John Hufnagel almost from the first snap of the season, and rode it with the intensity of a jockey on the lead driving the last sixteenth of a mile in the Kentucky Derby. Joe Paterno, subtle as a crowbar, told the writers after a particularly good performance by Hufnagel in a game against Boston College, "I think you saw the Heisman Trophy winner out there." The slogan was: Huffy for Heisman. Hufnagel finished up the track.

John Cappelletti probably merited pre-season Heisman noises. And the slogan was built in. John's summer job was hawking Italian water ice at a stand across from a playground and down the street from his family's Upper Darby home. What could be more natural than Iceman for Heisman?

The publicity department, however, had been burned the year before. So it let Cappelletti's stats to the drum-beating. And down the stretch, Cappy played the percussion set with the loudness that would earn him a spot on any of today's heavy-metal rock groups.

Vs. Army: 17 carries, 151 yards.

Vs. West Virginia: 130 rushing yards, four touchdowns.

Vs. Maryland: 202 yards on a school-record 37 rushes.

Vs. N.C. State: 220 yards and three TD's in a school-record 41 carries.

Vs. Ohio U: 204 yards and four TD's.

John Cappelletti . . . the 1973 Heisman Trophy winner.

The statistics were extremely impressive. The opponents at the time were not. Cappelletti won the Heisman by a mile. Penn State struggled to crack the nation's top five despite an 11-0 record and a roster that included 19 future National Football League players.

"I think we could have been the best team in the country," Cappelletti said. "I don't see anyone else who could have been that much better—if better at all. But Notre Dame beat Alabama in the Sugar Bowl and I think the emphasis was on that one game. There just wasn't much we could do. We didn't get into the right situation in the bowl picture."

The Lions found themselves squeezed out of the number-one picture. Ohio State and Southern Cal had to play in the Rose Bowl. ABC-TV had the Sugar Bowl, matching unbeatens Alabama and Notre Dame and dutifully pumped it up as the greatest match since Athens vs. Sparta. Penn State had to settle for a match with Lousiana State, a two-touchdown loser to Alabama at home in its next-to-last game of the season after a 9-0 start and, worse, an upset loser to Tulane in the regular-season finale. The Lions won the match, 16-9, although Cappelletti was held to 50 yards in 26 carries.

Still, the future loomed brightly. Cappy was a first-round choice of the Los Angeles Rams, the 11th player chosen overall. His first year he sat and learned. His second he scored every eight times he touched the ball as the designated goal-line plunger. And then he started all 42 games over the next three seasons. His stats were not spectacular. In 1976, his most productive year, he ran for 688 yards and a 3.9 average and caught 30 passes for a 10.1 rate. But many a block opened the way for Lawrence McCutchen to turn three yards into ten.

"I'm sure a lot of people look at my career and question the fact that I was the Heisman Trophy winner," John said. "But they are looking for that specific moment that you look for when you are studying someone who is just explosive. I'm not the explosive type. I'm more day-to-day, work hard and try to get the job done."

These are the words of a child of your basic work ethic background. Dad still works his full shift moving and setting heavy machinery. Mom still runs the water ice stand she helped her son set up when Iceman for Heisman was a dream instead of a memory. The schedule this year says 14 games and you're a starter, so you start in all 14 games and forget the bumps and bruises.

And then, in 1979, John Cappelletti couldn't answer the bell. And his past came back to haunt him. The guy who was always around was told by the medical people to take the year off. And for good reason. Torn muscle in the pelvic area had rendered his right leg useless as far as carrying a football past a professional defense. Or a high school defense, probably. So John listened to the doctors who told him to abstain. And then he listened to the critics who questioned his loyalty and team spirit. Either way, he was damned.

"I think that's something that happened and doesn't have to be talked about too much," John said. "The point was, I think, that I was listening to people who were telling me what I should be doing. I was doing what the team physician and the trainers were telling me I should be doing, which was basically take the year off. There was nothing they could do for me as far as rehabilitation.

"I think the problem came about when I started coming to practice or to a game and came away with the feeling that I didn't want to do that. I didn't want to be just hanging around when everybody else was doing his job and I was just sitting there, not having anything to do. I felt I could use my time better. And I think that's where the problem cropped up. People said I didn't show up a lot of the time so I wasn't part of the team. Well, I wasn't able to contribute so I didn't feel like I was part of the team."

He was caught in the middle. He felt conspicuous by his presence. Others in the Rams' official party felt him conspicuous by his absence. The Rams made the Super Bowl. Cappy made the controversy list. Apparently some things are bound to happen only once in a lifetime. You just read about two of them.

"I considered how I felt, but I guess I failed to consider how other people might feel I should still be there as a support-type thing," Cappy said. "Maybe I was looking at it selfishly, but to be hanging around and not doing anything didn't seem to me the best way I could spend my time. I had gone back that pre-season with the injury. I tried to play, but I don't think I lasted a week. I could not pull my leg around, not with the muscle all gone. There was nothing left to help pick up my leg."

John Cappelletti spent the year away from the sidelines and heard the snide lines. And then he moved to the San Diego Chargers. Grind-it-out, Cappy, meet Air Coryell! This was Arlo Guthrie's "City of New Orleans" in living color. The Broadway Limited joining the Concorde.

Except this time, the train didn't die. The Air Force realized its ground cover had value. Cappelletti struggled through an indefinite exhibition season, made the Chargers and ran the ball for 364 yards, a 3.6 average that mirrored the rest of his pro career and five touchdowns.

"Even though I had taken off a whole year and even though I had worked hard to rehabilitate the leg because I wanted to come back, I had a very difficult time that pre-season," John remembered. "I wasn't 100 percent sure if I was going to be able to last through the season. I just took it easy when the leg felt bad and worked it hard when it felt good and it worked out fine."

It kept working out fine in 1981. This year, Cappelletti got to play a significant role in the Game That Wouldn't End. It was the AFC playoffs, round one, San Diego at Miami. It had its unforgettable moments (the lateral at the end of the first half that glued four time zones to the TV screen for the never-ending replays) and its forgettable moments (potentially-winning field goals

John Cappelletti . . . today, as a running back with the San Diego Chargers.

floating two time zones wide left). And when it was over, it would go down as the greatest game in professional football history until a future one argued the point.

Which is where we leave John Cappelletti—married to hometown Upper Darby, Pa., Betty: father of two-year-old son Nicholas and, perhaps the one football player who has experienced everything but the Super Bowl, and that by a technicality.

Who else, from an independent college, spent his sophomore New Year's in Dallas, his junior one in New Orleans and his senior one in Miami? And played in the professional football game that will command more highlight footage than any other one?

Forget the 1971 Sugar Bowl, which he missed. Forget the 1979 Super Bowl, which he missed. Each time, it wasn't his fault. Remember instead, that December night in 1973 when he dedicated a nationally-important award to a chubby, round-faced 11-year-old who demanded love by his presence.

Archbishop Fulton J. Sheen was right.

John and Joey Cappelletti both won the Heisman Trophy that night.

Steve Suhey, himself a first string All-America selection at guard for Penn State in 1947, had three sons play for Penn State—Larry, Paul, and Matt.

4

ALL IN THE FAMILY

Featuring The Suheys

F or John Cappelletti, four years at Penn State was a positive experience. "I can only remember one or two bad times," he said. "Other than that, if I had it to do over again, I would do it again. And I certainly could recommend the school to someone else. It worked out fine for me, even without all the little extra things that happened to me as a senior."

But what of Michael Cappelletti, John's younger brother who was a freshman on campus when all those little extra things were happening to Big John? Mike was tough as steel wool, but size was his natural enemy at the Penn State level of competition. He spent two varsity seasons at linebacker, then asked Joe Paterno to switch him to tailback—John's old position—as a senior. Paterno complied, but Mike got little offensive playing time. He carried the ball twice, gained three yards and learned how Tommie Aaron must feel, being the trick part of the trivia question: What set of brothers holds the major league record for home runs?

"I think he was disappointed that he didn't get to play more, and it was difficult for Michael to follow me up there," John said. "He was a borderline player at that level, but he still got as much as he could out of the school. He still goes up there an awful lot. He likes it up there. He's made a lot of friends in that area, and he got an education out of it. He got his degree. That's a difference, too. Even the guys who don't become starters and so-called stars can benefit through the other parts of the college if they have the desire to do it."

The Golden Years of football in Lion Country have been flecked with family acts. Jim Garrity led the Nittany Lions in receptions with 30 in 1953; nearly three decades later his son, Greg, became one of Paterno's valued receivers.

(from left) Steve Suhey, Bob Higgins and Ed Czekaj.

Ginger Higgins Suhey, wife of All-America Steve and mother of Nittany Lion players Larry, Paul and Matt, sits with her late father, longtime Penn State football coach Bob Higgins.

Andy Drazenovich was only 5 9-1/2 and 195 pounds when the walk-on did all the long snapping for the 1978 team that almost won the national championship; his dad, Joe, and uncle, Chuck, were Penn State footballers in the late 1940's. In fact, Chuck, a linebacker of considerable ability, later had a 10-year career with the Washington Redskins.

Future pro football Hall of Famer Franco Harris never made All-America at Penn State, but kid brother Pete did after leading the nation with 10 interceptions as a junior, and Guiseppe also followed his two brothers to Lion Country. The first two black players at Penn State were brothers Dave and Harry Alston.

Walt Bahr never played at Penn State, but he became the school's soccer coach and contributed future NFL sons Chris and Matt to the football program where both did kickin' right. And Pitt will never forgive Dr. Sam Bradley, a Johnstown dentist, for letting his sons, Jim, Tom and Matt, escape to University Park. Elwood Petchel threw two touchdown passes in the 1948 Cotton Bowl, then went back to Dallas 27 years later to see his son, Woody, play in the same game.

Tony Orsini, a running back for the Lions in 1949 and 1950, sent an older son to Notre Dame, a younger son to Temple and a middle son, Mike, to his alma mater.

Some other brother combos include Dennis and Andy Onkotz, John and George Reihner, Dave and Rob Shukri, Bob and Rick Knechtel, John and George Kulka and Ron and Craig Coder.

And do you know when the Nittany Lions' stunning 48-14 upset of top ranked Pitt in 1981 was born? Probably in the spring of 1980 when Paterno convinced the top wide receiver prospect in the nation, Kenny Jackson, to sign on the dotted line. It was then that Kenny asked Joe if there was a chance that he might be interested in brother Roger, who was in a New Jersey junior college near home. Paterno said he would check Roger out. The nation checked Roger out on television in the Pitt game when his incredible interception in the end zone was the pivotal play in turning a 14-point deficit into a 34-point victory.

You talk about Penn State football and families, though, and one person comes to mind above all others. Did the person play football for Penn State? No, she didn't. But Ginger Higgins Suhey watched enough of it—three generations worth, in fact. She watched her father coach it and her husband and sons play it. The streak ended in 1979 when youngest son Matt played his last game for the Nittany Lions. Or did it?

Ginger Suhey is pointing to a picture on her living room wall. It is of her daughter Kathy's son. "Well, this little fella is pretty active," Ginger said in a voice that held hope for a fourth generation of Penn State football.

* * * * *

The calendar was telling a lie, something not all that unusual in Happy Valley. The time was late March; the guy on the radio said an inch or two of snow and ice were on the way. Ginger Suhey wasn't going to let it bother her. By noon, she would be in her car with a friend from town on her way to Williamsburg, Va., where colonial history abounds and it never snows in late March.

We are in the living room of the pleasant home on Sparks St., in State College. There is a field, the only thing that separates the backyard from State College High where Larry, Paul and Matt Suhey starred in football and wrestling. From the street, you can see the middle school that the future Penn Staters attended.

The house is filled with football memories, but by no means was football considered a foregone conclusion for the Suhey sons, Ginger says. In fact, she adds, the boys were not steered in any way toward the game by their father, Steve, an All-American lineman for Penn State in the late 1940's and later for the Pittsburgh Steelers.

Paul Suhey, who is a student at the Philadelpia College of Osteopathy, agrees with his mom about the subordinate role football had in the early upbringing of himself and his brothers.

"I never knew my dad even played football or was an All-American until I saw his picture one day on the wall at Rec Hall," Paul said. "I just got into athletics on my own. In fact, my brother Larry was a much bigger influence on my getting into football and wrestling than my father. Larry had some success at both sports and he was three years older than I was, so it just naturally followed that I get involved.

"And I never felt that I **had** to go to Penn State because my father had gone or because my brother had gone. In fact, I had thought seriously about going away to school."

It was the thought of being away from State College that drove Steve out of the coaching business four years after the end of his pro career. That and the fact that it wasn't easy making ends meet with a teacher/coach's paycheck and lots of little hungry mouths waiting at home.

As for Ginger, State College was all she had ever remembered. Her father had won All-America honors on Walter Camp's 1919 squad, then had gone off to coach at West Virginia Wesleyan and Washington University of St. Louis. In 1929, when Ginger was two years old, Bob Higgins returned to Penn State as an assistant to the legendary Hugo Bezdek. A year later, the university board of trustees booted Bezdek upstairs, probably as much for his inability to beat Pitt more than once in 12 years as anything else. In March of 1930, Bob Higgins was named head football coach at his alma mater.

Throughout his tenure as Nittany Lion coach, Higgins labored under the awesome burden of trying to play a big-time schedule without athletic scholarships. In his first nine seasons, the team was able to break above .500 only once. But the 1939 season brought a 5-1-2 season, capped by a satisfying 10-0 win over Pitt, and the Nittany Lions were on their way to a succession of non-losing campaigns that remains unbroken.

"So football has really been a way of life for our whole family," Ginger Suhey said. "Every year of my life, someone in the immediate family has been involved with football.

"Being around a coach in football season is tough, especially when you are married to a high school coach, because high school coaches have to do so much. You teach all day and then you're the coach, trainer and everything else. So I think you have to be supportive.

"We didn't discuss football much when my father was coaching and when he came home after practice, because he was coming home to a houseful of women (a wife and three daughters). And that was probably a relief to him, that he didn't have to talk about more football. And when Steve or my dad came home after a particularly tough loss, the best thing you could do is just cook a good meal. But we all enjoyed it when my father coached. Of course there were times when people criticized and you had to shut your ears to it."

Growing up in Bob Higgins' home was also a slightly more crowded situation than the family had bargained for.

"When Steve first came to Penn State," Ginger remembered, "I was in high school. My mother and dad always kept some football players in the house.

"An alumnus named Dick Lowe was responsible for Steve coming to Penn State. His brother was principal of Cazenovia (N.Y.) High School, and they were both interested in having Steve come here. Steve had never been away from the Syracuse area, so coming here was a big step for him.

"Those, of course, were the days before scholarships. So, when the boys came, they either worked at the fraternity for their meals or they lived with the coaches. Mother and daddy used to keep anywhere from two to four. In those days, you didn't need as many football players on the team, because they played both ways. Now they have something like 100 grants. Then they had 35-40 players. But that's how Steve and I met in 1942. And when he came back from the service, we were both sophomores at Penn State."

In 1949, the year after her father retired as Penn State coach, Ginger and Steve were married before his second year with the Steelers.

Ginger taught at Pittsburgh's Springdale High while Steve played pro ball. But the family quickly grew. Steve, Jr., was born in 1950, Kathy in 1951, Betsy in 1952, Larry in 1954, Nancy in 1955, Paul in 1957 and Matt in 1958. Steve coached and taught and enjoyed both, but that career came to an end in Kingston, Pa.

"By that time, we had five children and it was kind of hard to live on a school teacher's salary," Ginger said. "But we had met a man who had this territory, selling jewelry to schools, class rings and things like that, and Steve decided to do this. I know a lot of people felt he was crazy but our feel-

(from left) The late Steve Suhey, son Larry, Woody Petchel and dad Elwood at the 1975 Cotton Bowl. The sons were getting ready to play Baylor; 27 years earlier the dads had tied SMU in Penn State's Breakthrough Bowl.

Matt Suhey (32), the second leading rusher in Penn State history, follows guard Marty Sierocinski (67) in the Miami game.

ing was, 'Why not try it, we can always go back into teaching.' Of course, those were the days when there were a lot more teaching positions than there are today. Plus, the move gave us an opportunity to come back to this area."

So the rapidly-growing Suhey family came home, Ginger to a father who was finding retirement a burden and Steve to a new job that would support the family, thanks to long hours and hard miles forcing an automobile up and down the winding mountain roads of Central Pennsylvania.

"My father was a really great guy," Ginger said. "Everybody loved him. He was a great big Irishman who had an awful lot of charisma. The boys really liked him, too—the players, I mean. They must have, or why would they have kept coming back? I think he tried to make football as much fun as possible. Of course, in those days, it was a lot different. It wasn't the big business that it is today. It was much more low key.

"But once he retired, my father had a very difficult time of it. If someone doesn't have a whole lot of hobbies, that can happen and football was his whole life. So I think he really didn't enjoy retirement that much. But he did enjoy going to the games and, even after he was paralyzed (via stroke), Steve took him to every single game. Every home game, he was up in the press box. He really looked forward to it. I think that made his whole year, looking forward to the fall.

"My father genuinely liked people. He was a real family person. I think he would have loved to have a boy, but maybe it was best that he didn't. My mother was a tiny woman, 5-2, and weighed maybe 90 pounds. And that's probably who the boy would have taken after, my mother."

Ginger Suhey breaks into her easy laugh. Now there are footsteps on the stairway. A large male in his 20's enters the living room. Large and familiar. Ron LaPointe won two letters as a Penn State tight end in the late 1970's and had a stint with the Baltimore Colts. Now he's back at Penn State, going to graduate school. He had been looking for a place to stay and, well, mother and daddy used to keep anywhere from two to four football players...

The more things change, the more they remain the same.

"Paul Johnson was from Cazenovia, just like Steve," Ginger Suhey said, recalling the super-quick flanker/defensive back from the late 1960's squads. "When Paul and his wife Judy came here, they were like our children. They had their little baby, Kara, at the time and they would baby-sit for us. We really didn't want to get a baby-sitter as such but we had to have someone here when we were away. Well, the kids loved them both. And Paul would work out with the kids, too, and you can't imagine what a thrill it is for a bunch of young high school players to have this great young college player to help them."

These were the times when Larry was on the verge of making his All-State mark at State College High in both football and wrestling. They were also the times when Steve Suhey, Jr., was ending his high school football career that he would not carry on to college. If it bothered Steve, Sr., he certainly fooled a lot of people.

"He never put any pressure on any of them," Ginger said. "If Larry or Paul or Matt hadn't wanted to play, I don't think it would have bothered Steve one way or the other. A lot of people force their children into doing things, but I don't think that's right at all. We always tried to stress the academics over football. Football, after all, is going to be over, but you have your whole life ahead of you.

"Steve was very knowledgeble, and when the boys came home from school and asked him about this or that, he would work with them—but only if they asked him. And in the pre-season, a whole bunch of kids would meet in our back yard and Steve would put them through drills and get them ready. He loved doing it.

"Steve always tried to keep things in their proper perspective. He was a taskmaster who said this was this and that was that, but he was very good with the boys."

And throughout Lion Country, it was always assumed that the Suhey boys would follow their father to Penn State. It turned out that way, but it was never predestined to take place.

"Larry always wanted to go to Penn State," Ginger Suhey remembered. "He was in wrestling and track, and sometimes when you're in other sports, you can't go running all around the country. Steve always wanted the boys to go where they wanted to go. So what he told them was this, 'If you're interested in going anyplace, pick four schools and concentrate on them,' which I think was a good philosophy because I think a lot of boys go all over the place and all they get out of it is confused.

"Steve and Larry went down to the University of Virginia and that was that. Paul was an exceptionally good student and this opened doors for him. He visited Maryland, Boston College and some of the Ivy League schools. The decision was a little more difficult for him. And for Matt, it was even more difficult because he was recruited by many more schools."

But they all stayed home in Lion Country.

Matt Suhey wound up his career as the second leading career rusher in the university's history with 2,818 yards. Paul Suhey completed a fine career at linebacker by being second leading tackler on the 1978 team. Larry Suhey's football career was shackled by injuries. He wound up with 268 rushing yards in 66 carries and a knee that constantly troubles him.

Steve Suhey went to the 1975 Cotton Bowl for a couple of reasons. One was to watch Larry play against Baylor. The second was to hold one more reunion with a special bunch of guys—the players from the Breakthrough Bowl, the 1948 Cotton Bowl that put Penn State on the national map. They had made it a point to meet every five years and reminisce about the pre-game near mutiny that probably brought them closer together as the years passed by.

This was not one of those five-year reunions, though, simply an extra one because it was in Dallas at the site of their game with SMU.

Steve and Larry Suhey posed for a picture with Elwood and Woody Petchel, two guys who had played in the 1948 game and two sons who would play together in the 1975 clash. It was the last time Steve Suhey got together with his old teammates. He died suddenly in January of 1977.

There was another man who was part of the Penn State family at the 1948 Cotton Bowl. His is an important tale in the history of Nittany Lion football. There were people in Dallas who didn't want him to be part of that team. They would have preferred if he had stayed home.

He didn't.

Dennie Hoggard as a Penn State senior in 1948.

5
DENNIE HOGGARD

The name of the magazine was Collier's. The United States was at war in two separate theaters at the time and a lot of the folks back home were reading magazines like Collier's and Life and Look and The Saturday Evening Post. They were oversized by today's standards, and glossier, too. And eventually they all disappeared from circulation in those forms.

Collier's was where Dennis Hoggard learned about Penn State.

"In the early summer of 1942, an article came out in Collier's magazine," Hoggard remembered. "The cover was a picture of Dave Alston. And he was projected to be the number one sophomore halfback in the country. He was a tremendous athlete. Physically he was built on the order of Jim Brown.

"In the spring of 1942—at that time freshmen were not allowed to play—in a scrimmage against Navy, he took a tremendous physical beating. But he was the kind of fellow who would never complain. When he got back to campus, he went to the infirmary a couple of times, but that was it.

"He had already scheduled a tonsillectomy for that summer, and nobody knew the extent of his internal injuries because he had never said anything about them. So he went in for the tonsillectomy and he never came out. And that hit State College like a thunderbolt.

"Now I had heard of Dave. He was All-State, All-World. He was from Midland, Pa., and he had a brother named Harry who came along on his coattails, but Harry wasn't the player Dave was. He came in with Dave, but when Dave died, he dropped out. He just couldn't handle it."

But the picture and the article in Collier's stuck in Dennie Hoggard's mind. And, as a result of Dave Alston, first black Penn State football player and leading rusher on the university's freshman team, Hoggard developed an interest in Lion Country.

"Up to then," he said, "I didn't know where Penn State was. I thought maybe it was near Villanova (about ten miles west of the Hoggard homestead in West Philadelphia's Overbrook section), or just beyond Villanova. But after reading so much and hearing so much about Dave, I became interested in State."

And, in 1942, with Dave Alston dead and Harry gone home, Dennie Hoggard found himself as the only black man in the Nittany Lion football program and one of a fistful of blacks on campus. He was also one of the few Philadelphians playing for Bob Higgins, mainly because an alum named Casey Jones had taken to personally recruiting most of Higgins' players. And Jones was of the impression that the Allegheny Mountain range was the eastern border of the Commonwealth of Pennsylvania. Jones' recruiting was definitely geographically, not racially, motivated. He had, after all, persuaded the Alston brothers to leave their Ohio River steel community to play ball for the Nittany Lions.

"In Bob Higgins' time, we never had any recruiting down this way," Dennie Hoggard said from his Philadelphia Society Hill condominium. "Philadelphia and New Jersey were unheard of. Most of the players were from the coal mines, or out near Pittsburgh. And when I went up there in 1942, I was the only black on the team."

And the social times were different. Martin Luther King, Jr., was 13 years old and tired black ladies gave up their seats on Birmingham buses every day. In the North, people clucked about the segregation in the South and acted like Harlem didn't exist.

The Southern white often bragged that "we treat our Nigras good." The Northern white winced, but it still was understood that the black man who lived north of the Mason-Dixon Line knew his place. Which, if you happened to be black and in State College and in need of a haircut, wasn't at the barber shop around the corner.

"When I first went to Penn State," Dennie Hoggard recalled, "there were six black undergraduates on campus. All men. Four of us lived in the same house. And there was absolutely no black community. We had to get our haircuts in Tyrone (a town 26 miles to the south and west). No barber in State College would cut our hair. But it was not a prejudiced town.

"You have to remember this. We didn't have the problem the black kid has today. I went to a high school (Overbrook, which years later produced Wilt Chamberlain) that was all white. I didn't know black-white, didn't encounter it until I went in the service."

Dennie Hoggard helped fight World War II for three years. When he got back to Penn State, carrying a G.I. Bill in one hand and hoping to catch lots of footballs with the other, he was joined on the squad by another Philadelphia area black player fresh out of high school named Wally Tripplett. On January 1, 1948, those two would make history. But we're getting ahead of ourselves.

"With Wally, it was the same as with me," Hoggard explained. "Wally went to Cheltenham High (which years later produced Reggie Jackson) and it was 98 percent white when he went there. So the transition wasn't that difficult for Wally or for myself. When I went to State...well, I enjoyed it. I can honestly say that all my years at State, except for one incident at the Allen Tea Room, we never encountered any outward sign of prejudice in the town."

There were, however, other places, other situations. In the South, they played their bigotry hardball style, out on the front lawn.

MIAMI, FLORIDA, 1946:

"We had a game scheduled with the University of Miami in 1946," Hoggard said. "Coming up to that game, I had a broken thumb. It would have been easy for Hig (Higgins) to say to me, 'Stay home, Dennie, you can't play anyway.' The Miami people had already said that if Wally and I came, they would have to cancel the game. And they did cancel the game.

"The Hig was a fair man, a father-figure type. He wasn't a militant or a crusader, but he was a fair-minded person. He called me in because he knew that since I had been in the service and had been exposed to more things than Wally, I might have more answers than Wally might. And he said to me, 'What do you think of us going to Miami and not taking you and Wally?' And I said, 'Bob, what do you think of it? And, please, just keep in mind that I just came home from a three-year war.' And he said, 'That's enough, that's enough. I'm not gonna do it.'

"I think if I had wavered some, he might have said, 'Since you have a broken thumb, it's just Wally. And Wally doesn't start, so I can make excuses.' But when I threw it right back at him, he just said, 'Okay.' And I'm sure it was a disappointment to a lot of my teammates. They had to be looking forward to going to Miami. It would have been a great trip for them."

ANNAPOLIS, MARYLAND, 1946:

"This did happen, which upset me. We were playing Navy at Annapolis. Navy, by the way, was the dirtiest team we ever played. Navy was the only team we ever played that called us names. We played at West Virginia and there was none of that. We played Southern Methodist—and let me say this, too. You'll never meet a greater ballplayer or a greater gentleman than Doak Walker, I'll tell you. He went out of his way after the Cotton Bowl game to shake hands with Wally and to shake hands with me. He was a great player, a great competitor. He could do it all.

"But, getting back to the Navy incident, it was something like our seventh game of the year. We were 5-1. We got off the bus and walked into the hotel. We're standing there waiting for our room assignments and the hotel manager comes over and he's shuffling his feet. Turned out Wally and I had to stay in another hotel. And by then it was too late to make other arrangements.

"Obviously at the time I didn't know a thing about it. But the following Monday morning, I made a beeline to Bob Higgins' office, and he knew why I was coming. We had an uncomfortable half-hour session and I ended up telling him, 'Look, Bob, just don't let this happen again.' And he insisted that they had not anticipated the problem and when they realized it would happen, then it was too late to make a change in plans. But the bottom line was this: they stayed in one place and Wally and I stayed in another."

Which brings us back to Dallas and the Cotton Bowl and Doak Walker and integration. The 1946 Nittany Lions beat Navy, but lost to Pitt to finish with a 6-2 record. With the military veterans and the kids, State approached its 1947 season with gusto. It pitched six shutouts and scored 319 points while allowing just 27 on the way to a perfect 9-0 regular season.

"When our season ended," Dennie said, "there we were undefeated, untied and no place to go. I don't want to name a couple of players who did suggest that Wally and I might stay home, or agree to stay home, because I don't think it would be fair to them. I do want to name the players, though, who did say there was no way they'd go without us. John Nolan was one. He was the team captain. And Fran Rogel; Fran said, 'Hell, no, we don't go.' "

What happened was that the Cotton Bowl had come courting the Nittany Lions. Yes, the bowl officials said, they would be willing to be the first major Southern bowl game to include blacks among the players. No problem on the field. But, uh, off the field was another matter.

"When it came time for the Cotton Bowl," Hoggard said, "Bob knew what I would take and what Wally would take. We had that Navy experience behind us. And the blacks on the Cotton Bowl traveling squad were just Wally and myself. There was another black fellow on the team, a quarterback named Charlie Murray, but he didn't make the traveling squad for the Cotton Bowl.

"In Dallas, no hotel would take us. My only stipulation to Higgins was that I didn't care where the team stayed as long as we stayed together. So we stayed at a naval base, about 10-15 miles out. And this was ironic because the nucleus of this team was all ex-GI's. This was supposed to be a fun trip and here are these guys going right back into the service, more or less. So it was a very, very sorry bowl trip as far as the team was concerned. At least as far as the white fellas were concerned."

The ultimate irony was to happen in Dallas, where the colors of the U.S.—red, white and blue—emphasized white at the time. And guess who had the time of their lives. Wallace Tripplett and Dennie Hoggard, of course!

"There was a great deal made of Wally and me being the first blacks," Hoggard said. "You can imagine in Dallas that it was in the paper every day. We even had a reporter from the Pittsburgh Courier, Lem Graves, who traveled with us. He did interviews and sent reports back to the Courier, and the Tribune in Philadelphia picked them up (The Courier and Tribune served the black community in Pennsylvania's two largest cities).

"By the time we got to Dallas by train, the black community was waiting for us. We didn't get the full impact until about the second day we were there. When we arrived at the train station, most of the crowd was white. We were put on a bus and went straight to the camp. But Higgins and the camp guards were beseiged by blacks to see Wally and me.

"The second day he gave in. Wally and I went to the lounge and Hig said we could go to town, but that we had to be back by such-and-such a time. And he emphasized that we had to be back at such-and-such a time because we were getting special privileges, in effect, because he wasn't letting the white guys go out. So we went into town and that's when it hit us, the impact we were having.

"It was mostly people's houses that we went to, just house parties. One night we decided to go out on our own, to go to a movie. We had a key-to-the-city pass. We walked up to the cashier and she got all nervous and jerky and she called the manager, who happened to be from Pennsylvania. And he apologized. He said, 'No way can I let you come in and sit downstairs.' And he said, 'But if you want to sit up in the projection room with me, that'll be all right.' Now we didn't want to cause any trouble, so we went up with him to watch the movie. It turned out it was a movie we didn't want to see too much, so we spent more time talking with him than watching the movie.

"We went to church on Sunday. I forget the name of the church but the minister was Rev. Estelle. The people looked around at us and he told them who we were and they applauded. We sat in the balcony to the back, hoping that wouldn't happen, but it did. He happened to be a minister who knew his entire congregation and he sent his usher up to ask who we were. I guess we looked like football players and we were strangers. So you can see the impact we had on the Dallas black community. That trip was really a pleasant experience for me, and, I think, for Wally, too.

"The game itself was something else again. By the time that game was ready to be played, the coaches and the players, except for Wally and me, weren't speaking. Everybody was angry at each other. The Hig had kept a tight noose around them, wouldn't let them go to town. So they went over the fence, under the fence, through the fence. And then they just all decided to rebel together and go to town. Higgins got very upset with them and, by the day of the game, you could cut the tension with a knife. And that's the way we played in the first half, and we went to the locker room down by 13-0.

"Higgins came into the locker room and he said, 'The game plan doesn't have to change. Our attitude has to change.' He said, 'If you fellas can go back to Pennsylvania with your heads up high playing the way you played in the first half, then I don't want to know you.' And he turned around and left, and the (assistant) coaches, too.'

"And John Nolan, who was outspoken like that (Chet) Parlavecchio and very demonstrative, he got up and said, 'All right, you guys. I know some of you are mad at The Hig, but let's win this game for us.' And, in the second half, we went through Southern Methodist like paper. Marched right down the field, scored a touchdown, got the ball and went right down again. I know they would say they should have won the game, but the truth is that we should have won."

Penn State would have won the game, would have taken the first unbeaten and untied record back to Lion Country, except for a couple of factors. First, Ed Czekaj, later to become the university's athletic director, missed an extra-point placement that left the score at 13-13. Then Elwood Petchell, who had already thrown two touchdown passes, including one to Tripplett, tried to make Chuck Burkhart's long pass to Bobby Campbell only the second greatest in Penn State history. It was the last play of the game and the accounts of what happened are confusing. Some report that Hoggard flat-out dropped the pass in the end zone. Others, including that of the late Ridge Riley, Penn State's greatest football historian, point out that the ball was tipped and fell incomplete. Hoggard ascribes to Riley's theory. And he blames the first premise on broadcaster Byrum Saam, a Philadelphia legend who was the Penn State play-by-play announcer at the time.

"...the last play of the game, we had a 79-right," Dennie said. "But Elwood said, 'Everyone over the goal line. I'm going to throw the ball over the goal line.' Wally says he tipped the pass, says it hit his hands. The next thing I see, it's dropping to the ground and I dove for it and it went right off my fingers. Now Byrum Saam gave it over the air that the ball hit me in the chest and bounced off—and this is the way things stood. I didn't hear how it came over the radio until my father got me that night. My mother had gone to the game. My father phoned down. He had heard Byrum Saam's report and he knew how I hated to lose so he asked me how I felt. I told him that I didn't feel so bad and I told him what had happened, and then he understood. But most people remember it from what Byrum Saam said.

"The ball never touched me. It was tipped, and I think Wally was the one who tipped it. I was behind Wally. But when it dropped incomplete, the first person over to me—I was on my way off the field, I feel this hand on me, I look around and it's Doak Walker. He says, 'Nice game, you almost won it.' When I got to the locker room, I went to Earle Edwards, who was the end

Dennie Hoggard . . . today.

coach, and I said to him, 'Earle, when you see the pictures, you're going to be amazed. I almost caught that ball.' "

And thus ended the almost perfect season, fingertips short of fruition. The memories aren't elusive, though. This was a pack of GI's, battle-hardened in Europe and the Pacific, blending with a bunch of kids who learned about World War II through their hometown papers and radio stations. Together, at a school that didn't give athletic grants at the time, they almost pulled off the implausible dream.

And the two black players—Dennie Hoggard, the ex-serviceman, and Wally Tripplett, the man whose NFL career would be interrupted by Korea —were the microcosm.

"Wally was a great player," said Dennie. "Wally could have made today's teams, either offensively or defensively. People don't realize it but he still holds some pro records. The Sunday before he went into the service, he set a record for kick return yardage that still stands today."

There was also the guy with the tough Eastern European name and the tougher disposition who stood up for Tripplett.

"If I had to name the toughest guy on that team, it would be Chuck Drazenovich," Hoggard said. "He was a linebacker. The Navy game, they were calling us names. Nigger and like that. Chuck hears it and he starts hollering, 'Did I hear that? Am I hearing right?' This is Chuck, another outspoken guy.

"The words didn't bother Wally. When Wally was in a ball game, his mind was on the ball game. But, sure enough, the guy who's hollering the most is this Leon Bramlett, a defensive end from Mississippi. And Chuck knocked him out of the game. He decked him. Two or three plays after he asked Wally if he heard what he thought he heard, he wiped him out. Chuck was an undefeated heavyweight boxer at Penn State. He wasn't a great boxer, either, but when he hit you, my God, the whole place shook! And he popped that Bramlett, just rattled him."

The last year for Dennie Hoggard, Penn State finished 7-1-1 - defeated, tied and again uninvited. It would be Bob Higgins' last Nittany Lion squad. The Hig passed on in 1969. Too bad. He would have appreciated what has continued to happen to his dissention ridden Cotton Bowlers.

"I'll tell you one thing about the closeness of that team," Dennie Hoggard said. "We're scheduling a 35th reunion (on July 24, 1982). After the tenth year, we have met at least every five years. But things are changing. Steve Suhey is dead. Larry Cooney is dead. Larry Joe is not well. I hear that John Nolan is not well."

Life has changed for Hoggard since his Penn State days. He returned to Philadelphia, worked as a probation officer, then in the Department of Public Assistance. In 1955, he began work with the Philadelphia Board of Education. He has been there ever since. And, in 1957, he established his own jewelry business in West Philadelphia.

He is a widower whose three children are enjoying their own successes. And now he lives alone in the Hopkinson House, one of Philadelphia's finest addresses. Security is tight but friendly. Walk two blocks north, take a right and Independence Hall waves at you.

Walk that mile, up and back, in Hoggard's shoes and your feet feel splendid. We've come a long way, baby! Four decades ago, the man had to go to another county to get his hair trimmed. A few years later he and a teammate proved that, just because it was called the Cotton Bowl, it didn't have to be all white. Back home, he builds a successful business in one direction, a successful career in another. Dennie Hoggard pays his fees and nobody asks him to leave his condo. And surely nobody tells everyone in the building, "As long as **he** is part of your team, you're not welcome here." No one has suggested that the entire population of the Hopkinson House move to Fort Dix.

In 40 years, we have come to understand each other better. Black man and white man. Christian and Jew. Believer and atheist. The defense rests.

Would the prosecution like to cross-examine?

It sure would!

Lenny Moore rushed for 2,380 yards in three seasons for the Nittany Lions.

6
LENNY MOORE

They've called it the Laid Back Decade. World War II was a decade behind, Kent State a decade ahead. The 1950's were Ike and middle of the road and don't rock the boat. If you wanted to talk to Bob Dylan, you looked up his family in a Minnesota telephone directory under Z, for Zimmerman. And, if everybody had to get stoned, it was with 12-ounce bottles of beer that were called throwaways. Or, if you listened to The Hound on Buffalo's WKBW, which could be picked up practically anywhere, you got a little high on one of his biggest sponsors - Richard's Wild Irish Rose wine - while you listened to Bill Doggett play Honky Tonk, Part II, on the organ.

The Times, They Were A-Changin', subtly but definitely. And in no area was the change more pronounced than in the civil rights movement. In 1955, an exhausted black lady refused to give up her seat on a Montgomery, Ala., bus to a white man. She was arrested. A young minister named Dr. Martin Luther King, Jr. organized a black boycott of the city's transit system. Consciences in the North and South were stirred. "Bull" Connor became a symbol of repression instead of a peace officer. There would be no grey area around George Wallace—you considered him either patriot or villian. And major league baseball, which had been lilywhite before Jackie Robinson's 1947 debut with the Dodgers, saw its last bastion of segregation tumble in 1959 when the Boston Red Sox employed an infielder named Elijah Perry (Pumpsie) Green.

It was also the decade when one Lenny Moore went from Reading (Pa.) High School to Pennsylvania State University. Moore arrived at University Park when civil rights was a simmering pressure cooker, waiting to have its lid blown off.

Lenny Moore (center) with two men he loved—Penn State coach Rip Engle (left) and Reading High coach Andy Stopper.

The way Moore looks at it, the lid is still firmly in place today in State College.

"I knew nothing about Penn State until I went up to look at the college (in the spring of 1952)," Lenny remembers from behind his desk in the headquarters of the Baltimore Colts in Owing Mills, Md. "My first impression was that it was a gigantic place in the most beautiful area you would ever want to go. It was college life like you read about in books. Not like the University of Pennsylvania, sitting there in the middle of the city, or Temple. This was the most perfect collegiate atmosphere. I was just overwhelmed, really."

The whole world was indeed changing for the man they nicknamed the Reading Comet. Two years earlier, he started his junior year at Reading High on the bench. His academic interest was nil. College was the farthest thing from his mind.

"I was playing behind a fella named Ben Kemp," Lenny recalled. "Theo Mathias was a halfback. We were playing Steelton High and I'll never forget it because it changed my career. Steelton was beating us up pretty bad (they didn't nickname them the Steamrollers for nothing) and Ben Kemp and Andy Stopper, the head coach, got into a disagreement. Andy called on me and sent Ben Kemp to the bench. And Steelton continued to beat on me, just like they had beat on Ben Kemp. But that was the whole turnaround for me. If it wasn't for that, no college. I was small at the time and, I mean, I was solidly behind Ben Kemp."

By his senior year, Lenny Moore had gone from shrimp to star. He had a lot of college offers. Unfortunately, he did not have a lot of grades that colleges liked.

"I really didn't apply myself in high school," Moore freely admits. "At that time, most of my peers went right into the service out of high school, and that was because it took financial pressures off the family.

"I probably would have gone the same way. My brothers before me went into the serivce. But it got to the point where I was the only one in my family to have the opportunity to go to college, except that I hadn't even been thinking about going to college. You talk about role models! Hell, we never had any role models. Not for a black youngster. I mean, who could you look up to? There weren't any among the college ranks in those days. That was just the way it was. So I didn't have anyone I could emulate.

"We didn't have the use of television. There was no exposure for us. Very few youngsters at that particular time cared about school. It was just a question of what kind of job you were going to get, or were you going to go into the service, or whatever.

"There were 11 of us children and I was the youngest of the boys. There were two girls below me. And there's only three boys still alive today.

"I could have worked in school. There was no question I had the ability to do it. I just never had the motivation. But Penn State allowed me the opportunity to take the entrance examination. It was sink or swim, but I knew I could do it. It was just a matter of applying myself. I passed the entrance exam and off to State I went.

"I was in awe of everything I had seen on the way up. Your mouth hangs open, 'Wow, what a place!' And little did I know that it was the beginning of a lot of things, mainly an exposure to a completely different form of life.

"It's a shame. Much as I love Penn State and as much as I loved being there, being naive to a lot of things because I was young, there were things that just weren't right. Our little black group had to laugh off all the bigotry and all the racial policies there. You had to laugh it off or mentally fall under. So we made jokes about it, laughed at it.

"Each of us made jokes about how each other would react to different situations. That way we were able to make humor out of a very trying situation. Believe me, it was a heckuva learning tree with a lot of ups and downs mentally.

"There were some situations where I felt there were injustices even on the team. And I took a stand over it with Rip Engle, telling him that I didn't like the idea of him leaving one of the black players behind when he went on a trip. The player was Charlie Blockson. I said, 'Rip, you don't take Charlie and I'm not going.' But Charlie said, 'Len, you go. It's just one of those things. If that's the way it's supposed to be, that's the way it's gonna be.' So I went—very, very reluctantly, believe me.

"We knew we couldn't go to certain places in town, so we just stayed away. We knew we couldn't go in fraternities, so we just stayed away. We had to posture ourselves that way. And all the time I was there, I don't think we ever hit the hundred figure (in black student enrollment). We used to go to Altoona for our haircuts, but eventually there was a guy right across from the Rathskeller who used to cut our hair. We had one barber."

Which is one barber more than Dennie Hoggard had in his years in Lion Country. But the times were changing. Black people were questioning instead of accepting. When the questions weren't answered in a way that seemed proper, bitterness set in. And bitterness lingers longer than just about any human feeling.

When Penn State wooed Lydell Mitchell and Dave Bland, Dennie Hoggard was active in the recruiting. Don't, however, expect to see Lenny Moore trying to convince the next great Baltimore high school football star that Penn State is where he should continue his studies.

"Penn State hasn't really changed over the years," Moore said. "I just don't think they have made any concerted effort to change any of their old-line policies. It's strictly up to them to do what they want to do, but they just didn't do it. Because of this, I've never had any strong desire to assist them in any way."

"When schools like Alabama and Tennessee end up with more black athletes than Penn State, c'mon now, what are we talking about. That hurts me. Even when they played Alabama this past year, I think Alabama had more blacks on its team than Penn State did. That really hurt!

"Despite all the negatives that were there and that they never addressed, you couldn't help but love the place because it was so gorgeous. But it's strictly for the old-line white. There's just no place for blacks. I mean, if you were to ask me where would be the absolutely ideal community where you would want to be, the most peaceful kind of community, I would say I've never seen a place like State College. My, what a gorgeous place to live! Same houses, same stores—and the same traditions that they just will not change."

One year at Penn State, Lenny Moore roomed with Jesse Arnelle, a black man who was a fantastic athlete and was also a scholar. If Moore went to Penn State wondering what he was doing going to college at all, Arnelle had it figured out long before he touched down in Lion Country. In 1954, he carried the basketball team to the NCAA Final Four in the spring and was a big influence on a football team that went 7-2 in the fall. He went to law school and is now an attorney in San Francisco and a member of the Penn State Board of Trustees.

He is also a man who told the school when he was in line to receive an award in the 1970's that he and his old roommate have much the same philosophies about their alma mater.

"I have to echo some of what Jesse said in his speech," Lenny said. "It's not a love-and-hate kind of thing, it's a love-and-wait situation. That was when he turned down that award and that was to signify that the folks up there had to be about the business of change. It's too great a university not to be held accountable for these kinds of actions. In this day and time, there's so much more that Penn State can do, but it hasn't made the effort. There's a lot of education some of those folks need up there to understand that there are vast differences in the times and that their thinking has never changed. Their thinking hasn't progressed with the times, unfortunately.

"I was invited back in 1974 or 1975 and I addressed a group up there. I had been away from the university for 20 years. So I went on to tell them that it was nice to come back but that I too echoed some of the same thoughts that Jesse did. I said until there are some changes made in administrational policies, until some of those old folks stepped down, things could never change.

"And I had to address old Rip, a man whom I love. And I really have to believe to this day that Rip was naive to black-white relationships. I go back to any situations we might have had with Rip, and I have to be honest with you, I find no wrong in the man. I found the man to be honest, which is a trait

Rosie Grier threw the discus at Penn State when he wasn't helping Lenny Moore lead Rip Engle's Nittany Lions to another winning season.

very few people have in this day and age. He was very honest and trustworthy. I just love the man. He was always fair with me. I've always had the utmost respect for Rip, and I can't say there were many others I felt the same about.

"I like Joe (Paterno). I still do. And I'm surprised that there haven't been more changes with his power. He speaks good words with his philosophy, but it seems there's double standard there somewhere. Nobody's saying numbers, but Penn State down through the years has been out of line. They just haven't made any concerted effort, and don't give me the stuff that blacks are not educationally qualified. Bullcrap! And they know it at Penn State as well as anyone else. They're just jumping for excuses."

Probably the thing that most rankles Lenny Moore is that he and Arnelle tried a few years back to arrange a meeting with Joe Paterno, and it never happened.

"We've talked about it many, many times, trying to get a group together and go up there and sit with Joe, if he'll have our ear, to see what we can do to help him in his recruiting efforts to try and get more black ballplayers up there," Lenny said. "I tried to get hold of Joe, but Joe never responded to me. I called Joe's secretary to see if I could speak to him. His reply came to me third party, Jim Tarman (then assistant athletic director) called Ernie Accorsi (Colts assistant general manager) and asked him to give me the message. And I never responded to him again because that completely turned me off. I said, 'To hell with it.' And I wasn't begging for anything, only offering my services in an area where I think they have been dropping the ball up there for too many years."

Nobody ever accused Lenny Moore of dropping the ball very often when he was playing at Penn state. He rushed for 2,380 yards in three seasons, but tacked on only 89 yards in pass receptions, which seems strange in that he caught 363 passes for 6,039 yards in his dozen brilliant pro seasons with the Colts. Both figures are second on the all-time Baltimore records.

For years, people asked Engle why he never threw passes to Moore, considering what he was doing for the Colts. Rip's reply was lame: "He's got those stubby little fingers!" Fact: Moore has hands that would do a blacksmith proud. Truth: Engle didn't like to throw the ball to anyone. He held a charter subscription to Woody Hayes' philosophy, "When you put the ball in the air, three things can happen and two of them are bad." His idea of exciting football was a 70-yard scoring drive in 19 plays—18 runs and a pass. And who is to argue? He was, after all, six points richer when it was over.

So, most of the time, Lenny Moore ran with the ball. He gained 100 or more yards in 11 games. Unfortunately he never gained over 100 yards in a bowl game because the Lions never were extended a bowl invitation in his three varsity seasons, including a junior year when the team went 7-2. One of the losses was to Texas Christian at Fort Worth. The previous season the Lions had beaten the highly-regarded Horned Frogs.

"We really looked forward to that game," Lenny said. "People were talking about a match-up—me and (TCU star) Ronald Clinkscale. And it was kind of a test because I broke loose on one of those quick handoff plays. I was going toward the middle of the field and I knew where Clinkscale was. I saw him turn around and head after me. And I said, 'I know what this cat can do.' I kept him in my peripheral vision. I did make it over the goal line, but he was closing on me.

"The next year we went down there and that was another game we were looking forward to because we hadn't played in that area before. No blacks had ever played in Fort Worth Stadium at the time.

"We had all kinds of slurs hurled at us down there, niggers and whatever, and we should have won the game but we didn't. Anyway, I got the nicest letter from a white lady down there. I probably still have it at home. She said she felt a certain amount of disgust toward the way some of their fans reacted to our being there and playing the game. She said in spite of what had happened, there are Texans who don't feel that way. And, at the time, that was a letter that was really needed.

"The big rivalries were Syracuse because of Jim Brown being there. We beat Syracuse all three years (1953-54-55). But we never beat West Virginia when I was there, and West Virginia hasn't beaten us ever since. Huff was on those teams. Pitt beat us our senior year but we beat them the other two years. Those were the Big Four and in my four years no one ever beat the other three in the same season."

Toward the end of his senior year, Lenny Moore was pushed for All-America by the Penn State publicity department, which was understaffed. It probably didn't matter. Pushing a guy for All-America toward the end of his senior year is like announcing you would like to nominate your horse for the Preakness as the field hits the quarter pole. No chance!

Rosie Grier was a teammate of Moore's, another man who never received his proper praise until he turned pro. "Probably my junior year was our best team," Lenny said. "We had Rosie and Jesse and Jim Garrity and Don Malinak—all those folks. But we were an independent, stuck up there in little State College. Other than Harrisburg, we got no publicity.

In fact, last time I was back there, I stopped by Ripper's house. Rip and I got to talkin' and he said, 'You know, Lenny, I really feel bad after all these years that you were never picked for the College Football Hall of Fame.' He said he was going to continue submitting my name. But he said, 'We just didn't get the publicity. We didn't have a great publicity department and people just didn't know about us. It wasn't until after you and Rosie left that the doors started opening up.' "

The publicity doors opened up quickly in the pros for Lenny Moore. He was the first draft choice of the Colts. He made the Pro Bowl as a rookie, was All Pro by his third season. Baltimore won two NFL titles while he was there. And there are some who will insist that Lenny played in the greatest football game in history—the sudden-death victory for the title over the Giants in 1958. Moore disagrees.

"An earlier game that season was the best game we ever played as a unit," he said. "That was when we beat the 49ers to win the Western Division title. We were down, 27-7, at halftime against Tittle and Joe Perry and McElhenny and those folks and we came back to beat them, 35-27, to clinch it. That was the greatest game we ever played as a unit because everything had to be perfect. They had the ball; we had to take it back from them and then we had to score. Big Daddy and the rest of 'em went to work in the second half, Johnny Unitas kept taking advantage of them and we kept going down and scoring. At halftime, nobody in our locker room thought we were out of it. We knew it was going to be damn tough to beat them, but we felt to a man we could. There was no extra excitement in the locker room. Weeb (Ewbank) said, 'Hey, we've got to score four times and they can't score. It's just that simple!

"And that's exactly what we did. And from there, there just was no looking back.

"The Giant game, which everybody seems to say was the greatest game in history, that only because it was the first overtime game we should have washed them out in the first half. We had them down, 14-3, and we were going in for our third score, but we didn't get in before halftime. And then they came back and we had to fight for our lives. But we really put our own selves in trouble.

"You know, all those big years in Baltimore, we never knew why we were so great. It's only when we get together at our alumni gatherings and reflect back on it that we realize it now. We had a pretty damn good ball club—Big Daddy, Gino Marchetti, Brasse, Unitas, Ameche, Raymond Berry, Mutscheller, Jim Parker, Plunkett, Johnny Sample, Milt Davis, Szymanski. My, oh, my, oh my, what ballplayers!"

When Lenny's career ended in 1968, he found some doors still closed, others only partially open. Like television. Moore served for one year as color commentator for the Columbia Broadcasting System. He figures that he signed his own pink slip.

"I think it was only one year because of my initial reaction," he said. "At the last production meeting we had for all the color men and the announcers, one of the guys ended up with one of those nigger jokes. So I waited for him outside. Of course, the others watched me to see what I was going to do. It was natural, them knowing I was the first to do that kind of thing with no train-ing, no nothing. And I just let him know that whatever his reasons were, that he better not do it around me again. I told him, 'I'm not one of those who will grin and bear a blatant thing like that.' And I walked away from him. I might have signed my thing right there, but it was a matter of principle and it had to be done even though it might have cost me.

"I found out later that they had trained Gifford, trained Summerall. Me, they just threw in there. I had never even had a headset on before."

A man who was well-spoken enough to be a television analyst figured he had some kind of future doing commercials and endorsements. Lenny Moore was wrong there, too.

"I went to all the agencies in New York that year," he said. "You name 'em, I've been to 'em. I just wanted to let them know I was available. And I got, you know, pretty much the same story from all of them. One of them came right out and told me, 'Lenny, I'm going to be honest with you. The timing's not right for you. You understand what I'm saying?' And I replied, 'I under-stand fully and I appreciate your honesty.' "

The message was clear. O.J. Simpson would fly through airports and that was the end of that. As Lenny Moore loves to say whenever someone picks up positively on a point he has made, case closed!

"They always let one in the main door," he said. "Then they lock the door and nobody else gets in there."

Lenny Moore can quote you chapter and verse on the history of the black man's struggle in professional football, too.

"When I got to Baltimore, they operated under a close quota type of system," he said. "They didn't want the percentage to get too high. You could tell it easily. When they brought a certain percentage of blacks into camp, they never kept them around long enough to get a good look. If they started looking too good too fast, they cut 'em. Or they would pack 'em into the same positions so that one would cut the other. Over the years, it has changed—subtly."

Moore's first marriage produced four children and ended in divorce. His second ended in sorrow in 1975, the year he would become employed by the Colt's front office people and the year he was inducted into the Pro Football Hall of Fame.

"People often wonder why I have such vague memories of the induction ceremony," Moore said, "but within a month after it, my wife, Erma, died of cancer. I had more important things on my mind than an induction ceremony."

Moore is now remarried and lives in Baltimore with wife Edith. He knows that the color of his skin, which closed so many doors for him, opened the one with the Colts. His is the only black face you will see in the Colts front office, unless a player or coach happens to be walking through. His office is the first one on the right side of the hall. The title is Community Relations Director.

"Joe Thomas hired me," said Lenny of the former Colt general manager. "That's probably why I'm here, because Joe is very objective in his thinking. And thank goodness for him. He felt I could add something to the front office that they hadn't had, and he wanted me here. I started out in promotions. We had been running into an image problem. The team had sagged some and there were quite a few things the Colts weren't doing in the community that they had done over the years. We lacked that player-fan relationship. So it opened up the box for me to try to structure quite a few things."

The decision-makers are on the left side of the hall. Lenny is quick to tell you that he knows he'll never be invited to sit in on what happens on that side. But if you are starting to think that Moore's feelings about what's not happening at Penn State are just bitter remarks with no foundation, consider the following:

Three weeks after Moore offered these opinions, the NAACP called a press conference in State College. The group announced that it was thinking of filing a class-action suit against the University for what it called "insensitivity to its complaints of racial discrimination." The Rev. Gerald Loyd pointed out that, of the 11,500 employees of the university, only 232 were minorities. And of the student body population of 32,700, only about 740 are black.

"This is a climate not really conducive to good race relations," Loyd said.

On the other side of the Mason-Dixon Line, Lenny Moore was probably pounding his fist, gavel-like, on his desk and saying two words.

"Case closed!"

Richie Lucas was a 1st string All-American at quarterback for Penn State in 1959 and the runner up to LSU's Billy Cannon for the Heisman Trophy.

7
RICHIE LUCAS

In 1958, Jim Tarman was finishing his first year as Penn State's sports information director and Lenny Moore was winding up his third year as a Baltimore Colt running back. And Lenny, who couldn't get any All-America mention at Penn State, concluded the season in splendid fashion. He was named to the All-NFL team. The award was richly deserved. Moore had rushed for 598 yards and a 7.3 average. He had caught 50 passes. He had scored 14 touchdowns. And, in the infamous sudden death victory over the New York Giants, he had caught six passes for 101 yards.

Tarman knew a thoroughbred when he saw one. Had he been at Penn State when Lenny was running wild, he would have had Moore's picture in every paper in the country before his senior season even began. He would have found a way. And now Tarman had Richie Lucas approaching his senior year. He also had a quote from Rip Engle to the effect that Lucas was the best triple-threat quarterback in the country until someone showed the coach an athlete who could run, pass and punt better than Lucas. But Tarman needed a gimmick.

Looking back on it now, Lucas understands. Back then, he did not.

"You look at football on television now and you realize the publicity push is not the hype anymore," Lucas said from his office in Rec Hall. "Now it is the wide media exposure that puts players in the spotlight. You try to relate that to some of the things that happened when you were playing the game and you come to the realization that it is a completely different era.

Richie Lucas (33) looks for someone to block after handing ball to running back in 1959 game against Illinois in Cleveland's Municipal Stadium.

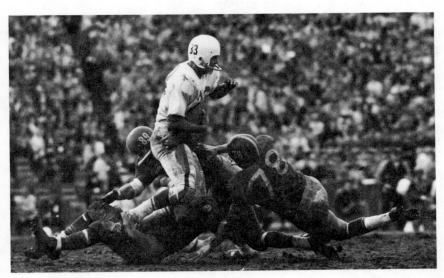

Three Pitt linemen attempt to stop Richie Lucas in the annual "Beast of the East" game—the East's greatest football rivalry.

"We went out and tried to do our best, but there really didn't seem to be much pressure on us. We were in the second part of the transitional period with the Lenny Moores and the Roosevelt Griers and the Milt Plums. I think we were only the next step in that progression, so we were somewhat underdogs.

"I think the school realized when it had Lenny Moore that there was something lacking. He could have been All-American with any kind of campaign. And Milt Plum did not receive the accolades that he perhaps deserved.

"I benefited from all that. They hired Jim Tarman and a whole new process set in."

And the process—build your hype before and not after the season—received its final boost from Al Clark, the crusty sports editor of the Harrisburg Patriot-News. Tarman had worked on Clark's staff briefly after his graduation from Gettysburg College, and now his old boss was on the phone, asking for something no sports editor would dare request two decades later.

"You're playing Missouri in your opener and Lucas made that gambling play last year that helped you win a game," Clark told Tarman. "Well, Missouri is riverboat country, so why don't you promote Richie as the riverboat gambler? Get a spread of pictures about it and send it to me. We'll use 'em."

Riverboat Richie. It had a positive ring to it. And so they dressed up Lucas in a derby hat and a vest and those elastic garters that fluffed the shirt at the biceps and a fistful of cards containing four aces. The riverboat image was complete. Not accurate, perhaps, but certainly effective.

It wasn't accurate because those majestic Mississippi riverboats like the Delta Queen only came as far north as Cincinnati, or occasionally Pittsburgh, at that time. In Pittsburgh, the mighty Ohio broke into two branches at the Golden Triangle. The Allegheny River headed north; the Monongahela went south, past the steel mills on its Pittsburgh banks, past McKeesport and then past Glassport.

Glassport was where Rickie Lucas grew up. The only boats that made their way past Glassport hauled steel, not vacationers. In Glassport, you made your money one of two ways. Either you worked for U.S. Steel or you worked someplace else, where the economy was totally dependent on the paychecks that came out of U.S. Steel. And when Richie was growing up, the paychecks were hardly a weekly regularity.

"My father was a steel worker," he said. "In that period of history, he was either laid off or on strike. I played Little League football and a lot of sandlot ball. In Glassport, that's what you grew up doing. We had excellent coaches and, in those days, you were very respective of coaches. You never talked back to your coach. You never turned around to say hello to your girlfriend. And if someone called out your name, you froze because you were afraid

Mary Ann and Richie Lucas as college sweethearts.

your coach might hear it. We had football, basketball and baseball in Glass-port, and if you played one sport you generally played all three.

"I was recruited as an offshoot. They were looking at a quarterback from Bethel High and they noticed me. His name was Jerry Eisaman and he decided to go to Kentucky at the last minute. I thought he was coming up here. But I was recruited by some other schools. I was invited to go to North Carolina State and to Miami (Fla.), but I wasn't much of a traveller. The only time I flew was when I visited the University of Cincinnati."

Finally he picked Penn State and used ground transportation to reach Lion Country. And once he arrived, he developed a very close working relationship with Rip Engle's offensive backfield coach, a man with thick glasses and broad-minded ideas named Joe Paterno.

"When I was 18 years old and 19 years old, I thought everybody was nice," Riverboat Richie remembered. "It was that naive position people brought with them when they moved to a higher level. Remember the idea years ago that athletes should be humble? I'm not sure that's true anymore. But Joe Paterno was just an unbelievably sensitive individual who was able to extract a helluva lot from you and made you feel good about everything you did.

"In those days, the quarterback was somewhat the leader in what we called the plays. We had to convey the image of leaders, so quarterbacks were seldom criticized in front of the whole squad. They were criticized and questioned at private meetings with the coaches. But now that they don't call the plays by themselves any more, I'm not sure they enjoy the same leadership position.

"You never questioned Joe, but you were always looking for the reason why he was suggesting things because you knew that he was always a step or two ahead of everybody else. I think every coaching staff should have a bachelor on it as an assistant because he can live and breathe football. I really think that coaching is something where your personal family is relegated to second position. Your squad is your first family.

"Joe was just a lovely person. Geez, I bet nobody's ever used that word about Joe before. Whether he knows it or not, he was just an authentic individual—authentic, straightforward, honest and with strong desires. You spent ten minutes with Joe and you felt good."

By the time Lucas' varsity career was over, it must have seemed like he had spent ten years with Paterno. Analysis by paralysis. Break down the films, offensive by offensive play. Why this call here? Why not the option there? Down and distance. Field position..Paterno the professor and Lucas the student.

"I played football for a long time before I came to Penn State and I never understood why I did certain things," Richie recalled. "Joe has a quarterback manual that was highly requested by a lot of schools. It was essentially why you did certain things at certain positions on the field. He broke it down into three categories—punting on third down, punting on fourth down and going for it on fourth down.

"After a ball game, at the Monday meeting, Joe would always ask me why I did certain things. You could always vary from Joe's quarterback manual if you had a good reason for it, or if you were using the element of surprise. As I remember it, we would give the ball to each of our halfbacks about the same number of times. In other words, seldom would I give the ball to one halfback 21 times and to the other seven times.

"Well, on one particular series, I forget our opponent, it was third down and a yard to go and we were in four-down territory. I decided to give the ball to Andy Maconyi. He was a nice guy but he was kind of spindly-legged, not really a power runner even though he was a fullback. And he didn't make it on third and one. So I gave the ball to Andy again on fourth and one, figuring, 'Well, he missed the chance for that self-satisfaction of being responsible for something positive. I'll give him a chance to make it up.'

"He didn't make it again, and Joe asked me about it on Monday. 'Why did you give the ball to Andy in that position, knowing his lack of power?' I said, 'Well, I thought the element of surprise would get them.' He was satisfied by that explanation, but he said, 'Okay, Richie, but when he didn't make it on third and one, why would you give it to him on fourth and one?' And I said, 'If they didn't think I'd give it to him on third and one, they sure as heck didn't think I'd give it to him on fourth and one.' The answer satisfied him. And Andy asked me about it many years later. He remembered that he had had a chance to do something responsible.

"But I've often thought that was one of the big differences between today and then. We didn't have anybody carry the ball 26 times in a game. I don't disagree with what they are doing today, but in those days I think it was more of a team concept, sharing the responsibilities of winning and losing.

"I was scared to death as a sophomore (when he made his deubt by replacing injured Al Jacks and helping the Lions handle hated Syracuse). We didn't have the opportunity to grow before we played in those days. We didn't have TV, didn't have the opportunity to see the pros the way the players do today. I remember asking (assistant coach) Frank Patrick, who had some pro experience, if he could get me some pro film, just so I could watch it. The opportunity to see someone perform at your chosen interest really helps you broaden your imagination, to imagine just how good you can be, but we were limited in our imagination.

"But it was a great era. Sometimes I think that everything has gotten too big, that the people in charge have lost control to television."

It is a stimulating thought, especially when you remember the following progression:

ITEM : In 1958, Lucas' junior year, Penn State made its first network television appearance in a regional telecast of a game against Boston University.

ITEM : The following year was the last for Penn State in cozy Beaver Field, which seated less than 30,000 and was located in the area of Rec Hall and the Nittany Lion Inn. After that season, it was dismantled, moved to the outskirts of campus and reassembled. Since then, it has been expanded to more than 83,000.

ITEM : The fourth quarter of the 1966 Penn State-Syracuse game at darkened Beaver Stadium was a rumor for those in attendance. The starting time had been pushed back to accommodate television.

ITEM : The 1968 Beaver Stadium game with Syracuse was cause for celebration for physicians who specialized in frostbite. The day was extremely raw, which was no surprise for anyone associated with Central Pennsylvania and December. The game had been moved from October 19 to accommodate television.

In a decade, the notion at Penn State and many other schools had gone from small-town thinking to "Take the television money and run."

"When I was playing, the stadium was right here," Lucas said, motioning out the window of his Rec Hall office. "It was nice in that I lived in the fraternity down the block and I was able to walk up for the pre-game meal and then walk back down to Phi Del. Even when we stayed overnight, we went to class on Saturday morning. They still do that.

"We used to get out to the ice rink on Friday nights before home games and there were 28 or 32 beds—bunk beds lined up one right next to the other—and it was considered an honor to be chosen to sleep there. It's not quite the same today, is it? Now our stadium is three times the size of what it was when I was in school and the satisfaction is that here we are, pretty much in the middle of nowhere, and we get that many people to come to our contests.

"And I'm not blaming TV, because it's been nice. But now there are too many pressures on a coach to succeed. I think Denny Crum put it awfully well a couple of years ago. He was talking about how he'd love to be loyal to his school, but the only way he could take care of his family is to put his name up to the next bidder. If he was successful at one school, then they weren't going to pay him any more until another school came along and offered him more money. The coach himself never gets a feeling of loyalty. Jackie Sherrill (who signed an immense contract with Texas A&M) is an example. Let's hope that doesn't happen too often. But he's a perfect example of how bad things can be.

"I think college athletics have a mission, and it's not what is happening today. The people who have a burning ambition to be teachers, to teach young people certain values in life, I think they may be a vanishing breed. I think some coaches are simply teaching how to win. And I think teaching how to win is taking some short cuts. Whereas at Penn State, I think the philosophy is that you teach people how to do the right things, the right drill, how

The Lucas family today: (clockwise, from left) Paige, Jeffery, Rich and Mary Ann.

to execute properly. And if you do enough right things, you're going to go out and win enough contests. Winning is the by-product of doing something hard and right.

"I think the greatest thing in the world is to see two teams go out there and have a hard game and have the players from both teams on the field talking to one another afterward, complimenting each other. Those coaches who bad-mouth an opponent after they get beat, it's kinda awkward. If they beat you and you bad-mouth them, that makes you a lot poorer than they are. I think you have to have respect for your opponents."

Which brings us to one of the great confrontations in Eastern football history. It happened in the seventh game of Richie Lucas' senior year. But perhaps we are getting a bit ahead of the story. This was the year of Riverboat Richie, remember?

"When I was woking in the steel mill between my junior and senior year, there was a lot of stuff about me in the sports magazines," Lucas said. "They started promoting me like they had never promoted anyone before. Everybody was telling me about it. I didn't read those magazines, but I was concerned about what it meant to the other players.

"I called Rip or Joe and said I was concerned. They said we could meet. And I said, 'I'd rather you didn't do that. I really enjoyed the fact that we had had a nice season the year before, but I don't believe what you are saying anyway and I wish you would stop it.' " And Joe's tongue in cheek answer was that they didn't believe it either.

"But like I said, that was a different era. I finished second in the voting for the Heisman Trophy and I didn't even know I was in the running for the Heisman Trophy. I found out about it coming back from someplace, I forget where. I didn't even know what this Heisman thing was at the time."

Maybe not, but Richie Lucas knew what Syracuse was. Penn State-Syracuse was The Game in the East that year. As usual, the coaches wouldn't even refer to each other by name. For feisty old Ben Schwartzwalder, Engle was "that blankity-blank down in Pennsylvania." And Schwalder's title was "that so-and-so up in Syracuse." The truth of the matter was that the two veteran coaches respected each other so much that they refused to admit it to anyone.

The season had started splendidly for the Nittany Lions. Despite one of the worst plane rides in post-Hindenberg air history, the Nittany Lions made it to Missouri and beat the Tigers, 19-8.

"What was that plane called, the Hawaiian Maiden?" Richie Lucas said. "Everybody has a different story about that trip. The pilot put a stick out front to prop the nose of the plane up while we boarded. Rip saw straw in the aisle and asked what team they had carried before us and they answered horses. (Some people remember Joe Paterno fastening his seat belt tightly for takeoff, forgetting it was on, deciding to stretch his legs once the plane was at cruising altitude and having the airplane seat join him in his upward thrust.) But we won the ballgame, strangely enough."

It wasn't really that strange when you noted that Lucas completed 10 of 11 passes against Missouri. And, in reality, the football team won twice that weekend. A United charter was ordered to replace the Hawaiian Maiden for the return trip.

While the team waited in the St. Louis airport for the charter to arrive, Tarman, ever the watchful publicist, grabbed at another opportunity to promote Riverboat Richie.

"He saw these large postcards with riverboats on them," Richie said, "so he bought some and we sent them to some people in the press (with handwritten notes from Richie, thanking the writers for all the nice things they were saying about him)."

A late fourth-quarter touchdown pass defeated Army and the Lions went to Cleveland to beat the Big Ten's Illinois in a game that excited the Lake Erie city about as much as water pollution.

Coming into the Syracuse game at Beaver Field, Penn State was 7-0 and the Orange 6-0. Schwartzwalder's team built a 20-6 lead, fought off a stirring Penn State rally for a 20-18 victory and went on to win the national championship. Penn State finished its 9-2 season by beating Alabama in the first Liberty Bowl.

"The Syracuse game was a good game and nobody minded the loss," Lucas said. "We played hard and we lost. Syracuse played hard and they won. That's the way it should be, the ideal way for a game to be played."

The game the rival American Football League and National Football League were playing was something else again. It was a dirty little war between the fresh new kid on the block and the one who had had absolute control up to then. They didn't shake hands and come out fighting at the bell. Instead, they threw sucker punches between the glares during the introductions.

"I was part of the first year of that war and I was drafted by the Washington Redskins and the Buffalo Bills (both on the first round)," Lucas remembered. "Buffalo indicated that I would have more of an opportunity to play quarterback up there. Plus, the Redskins were having problems. They were always changing coaches and the owner, George Preston Marshall, was always meddling into the running of the football team. So I signed with the Bills.

"I was a good defensive back. I could smell the football. I just had that sixth sense of knowing where the ball was going to go. But things have changed in that area, too. Today there is a lot more recognition of a defensive secondary player's talents than there was then.

"But I still wanted to play quarterback. In the NFL in those days, they usually gave you five years to develop into a pro quarterback, but the AFL got a little anxious.

"I played the first year and didn't do very well because of injuries. I went into the service that summer for a six-month (reserve) stint, and I was called back into the service during my second season because of the Berlin Crisis. That was the first football season in my life where I was involved in anything but football.

"I came back and was traded to Denver. But my wife had a baby when I was there. It was our first child and I was kinda homesick. Football didn't mean a whole lot to me at the time. My dad was either on strike or laid off, I had been out of school for three years and I was more concerned with security than pursuing the Denver thing.

"I came home and saw our baby (Jeffery, who is now 19; Lucas and wife Mary Ann also have a 13-year-old daughter Paige) and I got a job with Penn State in the Continuing Education field. And as soon as I got out of football, I didn't miss it.

"It always had been a game to me and pro football was no longer a game. You didn't have the concern with the individual athlete there like you had with Rip and the coaching staff at Penn State. All the assistants were special people to me and Rip was a special person himself. Rip to us was the father image and Joe was the big brother image.

Lucas is now Tarman's assistant. Jim has advanced to athletic director at Penn State, Rich is his assistant. And he seems to have no desire to ever leave Lion Country.

"You get trapped," Lucas said, meaning the good sense of the phrase. "State College is an easy place to like a lot, especially when you're raising a family. They call this Happy Valley and there's an awful lot of truth to that statement, especially in the sense that it is its own little world. It's a small town situation with the college atmosphere and I know my kids have really enjoyed growing up here."

Even though there's not even a river, much less a riverboat, within 30 miles.

Rip Engle and Glenn Ressler pose in front of a schedule devoid of Nebraska, Alabama and Notre Dame.

8
GLENN RESSLER

The entire area had little towns with strange names. To the west were Red Cross and Rebuck and Dornsife. To the south were Fearnot, Pillow, Hebe and Rough and Ready. Only to the north were there some fairly familiar names, like Sunbury and Shamokin.

Jim O'Hora, the Penn State assistant coach, must have visited half the villages mentioned above as he searched in vain for the Ressler farm in Leck Kill, Northumberland County, Pa. The world seemed full of two-lane roads to nowhere. Finally, a post office truck came chugging by. Yes, the letter carrier said, the Ressler farm was on his route, and if O'Hora wanted to follow, they would eventually get there.

And that is how Penn State found Glenn Ressler. Don't try to tell Jim O'Hora that State College is a place you can't get to, or he's liable to put you behind the wheel of his car and tell you to find Leck Kill. Everything is relative. For Glenn Ressler, State College might as well have been Los Angeles.

"I was going to the city," Ressler remembered about his arrival in Lion Country in the fall of 1960. "State College was a big town for me. Leck Kill, they had a post office and that was about it. Our place was just, I guess you would call it a general farm, a truck farm type operation. Some chickens and eggs and vegetables, that was about it. Like everyone else, we struggled by.

"It was a big thing when we got the telephone in the house, I remember that. And I can remember when we first got electricity. I was four years old. We never did have indoor plumbing, but it was just one of those things you grew up with and you didn't know any different. That was the way everyone

Casting a wary eye downfield at would-be Syracuse blockers, Penn State's Glen Ressler (63) pursues Orange ball carrier, quarterback Wally Mahle.

Glenn Ressler (left), with fellow Penn Staters Ed Czekaj and Sever Toretti, upon being inducted into the Pennsylvania Sports Hall of Fame in 1980.

else lived, too. Some of them were worse off than we were and some of them were a little better off. That's just the way you existed."

Glenn Ressler's existence has taken a large step up in class. The house is in Camp Hill, across the Susquehanna River from Harrisburg, close enough to the Interstate to allow Glenn daily access to his restaurant-chain headquarters 50 miles to the southwest in Chambersburg but far enough away from the highway that the shrill buzzing of speeding tractor-trailers can't be heard in the back yard.

There is a swimming pool in the back yard, which is on the top of a hill with a view so perfect that you swear all you would need was a pair of strong binoculars to be able to see State College, 90 miles away.

One of the walls in the family room is devoted to football. One of the pieces is a framed Sports Illustrated cover which showed Baltimore Colt number 62 helping to block the Dallas Cowboys as Jim O'Brien kicked the winning field goal in Super Bowl V.

Ressler spent his football life getting it done in the pits. Others have seasons filled with open field runs after handoffs or completed passes or interceptions. Glenn's career was push turning to shove, driving blocks and taped forearms. Grime was your constant companion.

"I went to Mahonoy Joint High School," Ressler said. "We didn't have any organized Little League football where I grew up. The first game I ever saw, I played in. I didn't know what the game was about. I had never seen football. We didn't have a television at home. When I was a freshman in high school, sometime I'd zip over to my neighbor's house to watch a game on TV, but I really didn't understand it.

"I guess I went out for the team because all my friends were going out for it. I remember earning my money to go to the football camp as a freshman. We had a camp up above Sunbury for a week and you paid your own way to go there. As freshman, I think there were four of us selected to go. I earned the money from picking strawberries. That's how I earned all my money as a boy—picking strawberries. Oh, man! I still have blisters on my back from picking strawberries. Also from picking potatoes.

"Like everyone else, I went out to be an end and a linebacker and it didn't take them long to make me a center. I played center, guard and tackle on offense in high school and tackle and linebacker on defense, and I carried that on into college. I've been a lineman all my life and I never scored a single point in my career."

No one, however, dare say he had a pointless career. Quite the opposite, in fact. He was a star almost from Day One. By the end of his senior season, he had attracted enough attention to be selected to play in the Pennsylvania Big 33 game. The big city of Harrisburg had discovered the big guy from Mahonoy Joint.

"At that point I started getting some college inquiries, but I was never heavily recruited," Ressler said. "The only other player out of our district to go to a major college to play football was Gary Collins, who went to Maryland (and later starred for the Cleveland Browns). He was four years ahead of me. So, obviously, we didn't get a whole lot of publicity. There were some good players and some of them went on to the state teacher college level of play, but no one except Collins had gone to a major college program. So, consequently, I was recruited only by Army, Wichita State and Penn State.

"I didn't have a lot of inquiries other than that. I don't know if that speaks well of me or not, but, like I say, at the time there weren't a great many players coming out of our school. We only had 83 in our graduating class.

"Jim O'Hora recruited me for Penn State, a wonderful man. I have the greatest respect for him. I visited Penn State with our phys ed teacher one weekend and pretty much made up my mind right there that I wanted to go. Before that, I knew as much about Penn State as I knew about any other college, which was nothing. In fact, I doubt that I would have gone to college without a football scholarship. I knew there were programs available, but I hadn't made up my mind what I wanted to do. I hadn't really given college much of a thought until my senior year in high school. But Penn State was close to home and when they offered, I just decided, 'That sounds good,' because it was a full scholarship, which would pay everything."

For a young man who had spent his life picking berries and potatoes to scrounge up a little spending money, a free ride seemed almost like too much to ask.

"I can remember picking 100 boxes of strawberries in a day, that was my record," Ressler said. "You'd get little quart boxes that you'd put on a flat, maybe six boxes to the flat. You'd fill your flat and you'd take it to the dump station and you'd pick up another flat and away you'd go. You'd try to beat out everyone else and get the best rows. That was our only real opportunity to earn money. It wasn't like today where kids get $8 to mow a lawn. In those days, if you got 50 cents and a candy bar for mowing a lawn, you were happy. Geez, that was a good day.

"I enjoyed Penn State, enjoyed the experience. But I wasn't sure it was the place for me when I walked in and saw the size of those fellas. Gosh, we had a lot of big players. But, fortunately, size doesn't tell anything about the caliber of players. The size of the heart, you can't measure.

"Coming from nowhere, Penn State was great. I had no trouble adjusting. I think the athletic department at Penn State helps the players adjust. They have study programs, tutor programs. One thing I will always say about Penn State, they always put education first among the ballplayers. They were more interested in making sure you got through your first year academically than putting the pressure on you to play ball. I think we only played three freshman games. And when I went to spring practice, I started out on the yellow shirts, which was the fifth team. By the time spring practice was over, I was on the green team, or third team. And when I came back in the fall for my sophomore year, I was second team. I played second-team guard my sophomore year."

By his junior season, Ressler was a middle guard on defense and, occasionally in short-yardage situations, a center on offense. And, in the next two seasons, the folks in Central Pennsylvania got to see plenty of him. Almost as much as the good citizens of Columbus, Ohio. In 1963, Penn State went into Ohio Stadium and scored a 10-7 victory, aided quite a bit by the fact that Ressler dominated Matt Snell, whose path he would cross again with quite a different outcome in Super Bowl III. Three times, Snell tried the middle of the line on fourth-and-short. Three times Ressler stuffed him short of the first down. It was hard to imagine Glenn surpassing his performance that day, but he did a year later at the same scene in the most shocking victory in Penn State history.

"We started out badly my senior year, lost four of our first five ball games," Ressler remembered. "By the time we got to Ohio State, they were ranked number one in the country. We weren't given much of a chance. In fact, people thought we would be lucky to come back from there intact, much less win the ball game. But things just fell in place. I probably had my best game as a college player. It was a case of playing up to our competition. We found ourselves surviving and suddenly we said to ourselves, 'Hey, these guys aren't that much better than we are.'

"It was just one of those games where everything went right for us. Every bounce went our way. We did have a good team but we just never really got it together until that Ohio State game. We absolutely dominated the game. In their defense, they did have some players hurt. I remember their starting center was hurt. And we had an outstanding quarterback in Gary Wydman and runners like Tom Urbanik, a big bruising fullback, and Gary Klingensmith and Don Kunit."

But nobody was as dominant as Glenn Ressler that afternoon. He personally harassed the Buckeye offense into one of the most embarrassing performances in their history. At halftime, Ohio State had no first downs, no completed passes and a total offense of minus-16 yards. The final score was 27-0 and Woody Hayes grumped afterwards, "They made one mistake all day and recovered it in the end zone for a touchdown."

And, in those short yardage situations, Ressler snapped the ball and blocked anything in his way.

"We had a few guys who played both ways beside myself," Ressler remembered. "Billy Bowes played both ways—he was an end. And I didn't play that much center, only in certain situations. And the regular center (Bob Andronici), well, they used to comment that he was the only player in the country who had an All-American for his backup. By my senior year, though, they were getting away from the two-way playing."

Life at Penn State had its funny moments for Ressler, too. Like any time Rip Engle decided to conduct the special teams phase of practice by himself.

"Rip was the organizer, but he was not the day-to-day coach," Ressler said. "Joe Paterno was the day-to-day coach. The only thing that Rip coached by himself in those days were the special teams. And he would get so frustrated that he would just get up and leave. And one of the assistants would come over and say. 'This is the way we're going to do it,' and then we'd get our kicking game in.

"It would never fail. All week Rip would come over and try to get our kicking game in, he would line us up and it would never go the way he wanted it to. We'd always screw it up. And we all kind of accepted it—'Okay, this is ten minutes when we've got Rip.' And after that period of time, we'd have one of the other coaches saying, 'All right, this is the way we're going to do it.'

"I'm sure Rip had an awful lot to say in the coaches meetings, but on the field he left an awful lot of the responsibility to Joe and the other assistants. I love Rip. I've never seen anyone who has so much charisma. And, oh, could he recruit! The families would come up and all he'd do is put on a little of the Engle charm on the mothers and that would be the end of it. That recruit was going to Penn State."

And eventually that recruit would get to see the flip side of Rip Engle as he stomped off the field, leaving his special teams in the hands of an assistant once again. Or he might get to see Garry Klingensmith go slightly offside. Kleingensmith was legally deaf, but he had some hearing ability, which he occasionally overestimated.

"He hated to accept the fact that he was deaf," Ressler remembered. "He could hear some things. So we're out playing at Oregon, and all week at practice, Gary would watch the ball. The ball would be snapped and he'd take off because he couldn't really hear the signals. Well, that particular week, he thought he was hearing the signals from the quarterback. I think the count was on two. Meanwhile, the defense starts yelling its signals. Gary thinks it's our quarterback and takes off down the field. Everybody else is holding his stance. Gary is 20 yards down the field before he realizes that nobody else has moved. And the coaches said, 'That's the end of it, Gary. From now on you watch the ball."

Jim Tarman remembers going up to Klingensmith after the game and telling him, "The official said that was the first time he ever saw anyone illegally in motion and offside on the same play."

Gary's answer was a classic: "Mr. Tarman, you've been telling people out here that we have a deaf player on the team. I just wanted them to find out who it was real quick."

Ressler also remembers lessons to be filed away for future reference.

"We were playing Holy Cross, which was not one of our stronger opponents, and Dan Radakovich was a defensive coach," he said. "Holy Cross was pushing us up and down the field. Dan said, 'We're going to have to get you guys out of there before you get yourselves killed.' He put the second unit in and the second unit kept pushing them back, pushing them back. I think it just points up to the fact that there are some games you just can't get yourself up for. People are amazed that a weaker team can beat a stronger team, but they don't seem to understand that the psychological factors are 180 degrees. If you're the powerhouse, there are times when you just can't get yourself prepared for another weaker team. You should be able to, but you can't."

Exhibit A: Super Bowl III

Ressler majored in agriculture at Penn State, but there is no truth to the rumor that Beaver Field was moved from the campus mainstream to a spot across a road from the animal barns to make it easier for Glenn to get from class to practice. Besides, Ressler has made absolutely nothing out of that phase of his education.

"I majored in it because it was my background and because I knew something about it," Ressler said. "but I've never really done anything in agriculture since I graduated. I still enjoy the concept of farming. My brother's a farmer. But I don't even put out a vegetable garden in the summer. I guess as a kid growing up, when it was understood I was going to do it, I did it. But I don't particularly care for it. When you are a kid, there are a lot of other things you'd rather do than take care of the farm. So I never really got that excited about being a green thumb."

Of course, he would have hardly had time to farm after college even if he had been interested, since pro football training camp begins in July and the season can continue into January. Ressler spent ten seasons working those months, and it's tough to harvest corn and block defenders at the same time.

But before the college draft was held, a couple more significant things happened to Ressler. For one, he was named an All-American. Also, the Maxwell Club named him college player of the year. And he was part of a group that did something no college team would even think of doing today.

"We probably could have beaten any team in the country my senior year after that Ohio State thing," he admitted, "and we certainly would have played anyone in the country—anywhere but the Gator Bowl."

But it was the Gator Bowl that came courting the Nittany Lions. And the team told the bowl officials to find someone else to take to the dance.

"We were given the option of going or not going to the Gator Bowl," Ressler said. "It wasn't like it is today. The team actually did the voting. And the team elected not to go. Needless to say, the university fathers-to-be were a little upset at us and that was the last time the players were given that option. There was a lot of money involved.

"We probably turned it down because, two years before, we had played in the Gator Bowl. We lost to Florida. So I guess it was something the players just weren't ready to do at the time. The training facilities were poor. We had trained at Annapolis for a week or two my sophomore year. There was the travel, the hassle. The seniors remembered it and, consequently, we elected not to go.

"As far as I was concerned, I had an opportunity to play in the East-West Shrine game, which at the time was a big game, and to go from there to the Hula Bowl. So, from a selfish standpoint on my part, I preferred to play in those two games than in the Gator Bowl. And I think most of us felt that the Gator Bowl was not a reward, just another three or four weeks of practice."

So Ressler went to the Shrine Bowl, where he impressed, and the Hula Bowl, where he impressed.

"I was drafted by both Denver and Baltimore and they both pretty much told me I'd be an offensive player," he said. "Baltimore had recognized me as far back as my sophomore year. We were playing at Maryland. The Colts had a player-personnel man there and he recognized me as a player who maybe had some potential. They kept an eye on me. And when I went to the College All-Star game in Chicago, they told them to play me on offense. I played some defense my first two years with the Colts, but it was just a spot thing.

"Pro ball was an enjoyable period in my life. I played ten years and the early part of my career I was fortunate that we were almost in the playoffs. But in 1971 and 1972, there was a lot of turmoil in Baltimore. That's when Joe Thomas came in and tore the team apart. And 1973 and 1974 were just disasters. I can sympathize with those poor players who go with teams that never have an opportunity to win. It's just God-awful. It's constant turmoil and players picking on each other and you're just waiting for the season to end. It's just not healthy."

Ressler played in two Super Bowls, losing the 1969 game to the Jets and winning the 1971 game from the Cowboys. He gives the 1969 team the edge in ability and winces over Super Bowl III.

"It was like the game never really happened," he says of the 16-7 loss to Joe Namath in Miami. "It was like waking up from a dream and saying, 'Well, that didn't really happen. It was a nightmare that didn't really happen.' That's how we all felt after playing that game. Except that it wasn't a nightmare. It actually happened.

"They had a good football team and, quite frankly, we underestimated them. We didn't think they were as good as they were. We had beaten some good teams in our league and we just felt like we had better personnel. But on that particular day, they proved us wrong. It was embarrassing. It's so difficult to get to the Super Bowl. And then to lose it? I just can't explain the feeling. But we were fortunate enough to be able to do something about it. And when we beat Dallas in 1971, we had a very good team.

"That was a hard-hitting game. It's easy to say it was a sloppy game with a lot of fumbles and a lot of mistakes. But the fumbles were just caused by physical play."

By that stage in his life, Ressler had already gotten involved in the restaurant business with his father in law. They began with a Red Barn franchise. Eventually they added six more Red Barns, and recently left the franchise and changed the name of the restaurants, which are spread between Lewistown, Pa., and Martinsburg, W. Va., to The Farm. Ressler also holds two Ponderosa family restaurant franchises. He is able to provide a comfortable life for his wife, Sandy, 12-year-old son Kevin and eight-year-old daughter Cami. And he says he will lead a very comfortable life himself if his son never never buckles a chin strap.

"I'm not going to put any pressure on him," Ressler said. "It's a difficult situation, because they're always going to compare him to the father and it's not fair to him. He has to make the decision. And, believe me, I'm not going to encourage him. It really doesn't matter to me that he participate in any sport. What is important to me is that he is a good student. And he is a good student.

"He plays soccer and likes it. I wouldn't let him play midget football. There's so much of a difference in size, and with developing bodies at that age, I just don't approve of midget football at all.

"I played the game for 18 years and never had a serious injury. I never had a broken bone, but I do have back problems and I'll live with that the rest of my life, jammed neck and all. After every pro game my last two seasons, I had an appointment with an osteopath to get my back put back in and my neck popped back out and it's not worth it. At the time, I guess football seemed very important, but when you look back at it, it's really not that important.

"I've seen too many fathers trying to live vicariously through their sons, pushing them into something that they're not really capable of doing and never will be capable of doing. And the abuse the child must feel! The psychological effects must be devastating when he doesn't measure up to what his father or parents expect. Because it's not only fathers. Mothers are just as bad. So I feel that's one pressure I don't have to put on my son."

The words are refreshing. The best football player Leck Kill ever produced isn't determined that his son will be the best football player Camp Hill ever produces. Glenn Ressler may have played football for 18 years in high school, college and the pros, but you know one thing for sure. He never played without a helmet.

Jack Ham, poised to make the tackle, was a 1st team All-America selection as a linebacker in 1970.

9
JACK HAM

They call Penn State Linebacker U. because of the great number of athletes the university has produced for the NFL at that position. Not that all of them played it in college. Dave Robinson, for instance, became one of the great linebackers in pro football history for the Green Bay Packers and the Washington Redskins, but he made All-American for the Nittany Lions in 1962 as a two-way end.

Matt Millen and Bruce Clark were recruited for Joe Paterno as linebackers but spent most of their football lives in Lion Country as defensive tackles who grumbled that they wanted to be back at their old positions. Millen finally got his wish—with the Oakland Raiders in 1979. All he did was help lead them to victory in Super Bowl XV.

Paterno even took one of his better offensive guards and made a linebacker out of him. Charlie Zapiec had spent two seasons on the Penn State offensive line. As a senior, he made the switch to linebacker and took to the position like a foodaholic takes to a buffet table. He chewed his way right onto the 1971 NEA All-American team before heading to Montreal and a long and productive career with the CFL Alouettes.

Penn State linebackers came from funny places. Dennis Onkotz was a short-punt-formation quarterback in high school, Greg Buttle was a tight end and Eddie O'Neil was a quarterback/safety. All three wound up on somebody's draft list and with considerable playing time in the pros, although Onkotz' career was cut short by a severe knee injury while a member of the New York Jets.

As usual, Jack Ham (33) was in the center of the action.

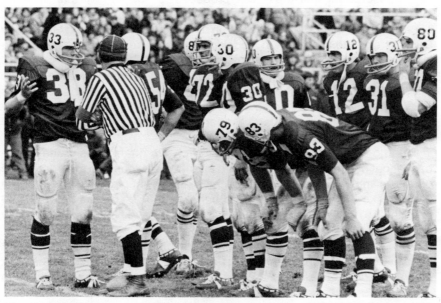

The Penn State defense has been penalized and captain Jack Ham (33) would like to know why.

And let us not forget that Onkotz and O'Neil both were punt returners in their careers. One of the great scenes of the Nittany Lion highlight film from the late 1960's was Onkotz, lineman's cow collar attached to his neck, dropping back to field a punt. How good was he at it? Three seasons, 47 returns, 619 yards, 15.3 average, two touchdowns. And Dennis wasn't a 4.4 40 man either, just an instinctive man in the open field who saw the wall of blockers before it even developed and ran to the spot where it would form.

Which is pretty much a Paterno Era portrait of the Penn State Linebacker. You asked the most defensive football players in the late 1960's and early 1970's the secret of excellence and the answer was, "You read, then react." But ask a Penn State linebacker the same question and his answer was, "You read and react." There is a fine line between the two statements and often it was the difference between a two-yard loss and an eight-yard gain. Two-yard-loss defenses are winners, eight-yard-gain defenses force coaches to type resumes.

The all-time Penn State Linebacker shared a lot of traits with his peers. He played a different position in high school, for instance. Once he pulled the Blue and White uniform on, he made reading and reacting a simultaneous happening. He was quick, as opposed to behemoth.

But there was one big difference. The others all had something at the beginning of their senior year in high school that Jack Ham didn't have.

All of them had starting positions on the football team.

Jack Ham has become a prototype. His clones include Lawrence Taylor of the Giants and Jerry Robinson of the Eagles, guys who will come from their outside linebacker spot and be on a quarterback's back on one play, then intercept him 30 yards downfield on the next. They are guys who roam laterally with incredible anticipation, fight off every play-by-play announcer's would-be blocker and make the tackle in the next county.

But back in 1966, Jack Ham was a would-be blocker, 160-pounds of offensive guard at Johnstown's Bishop McCort High School. There were plenty of college scouts around to watch McCort. After all, everyone was interested in Steve Smear, the tight end who would wind up as an outstanding Penn State defensive tackle but was blocked from All-American honors because the unwritten rule says don't take two from the same school at the same position. Mike Reid played alongside Steve Smear. Years later, Matt Millen would suffer the same injustice because he played alongside Bruce Clark.

The scouts might have missed Jack Ham early because he was on the McCort second unit. And they might have missed him late because 160-pound pulling guards are pretty much worthless at the college level.

"I wasn't recruited at all out of high school," Ham remembered. "I went to Massanutten Prep School, a military school in Virginia, for a year. And I was all set to go to VMI, which had offered me a scholarship. I had played pretty well at Massanutten, got some confidence in myself and built myself up to about 190 pounds. And late in the year, George Welsh, who was then on the Penn State staff, recruited me. Not very highly, though."

In fact, if the Nittany Lions gave out 30 scholarships that year, Ham was number 31.

"In late May, George Welsh offered me the scholarship," Ham said. "Someone else had turned it back and had decided to go someplace else. He had gone up for a weekend visit and changed his mind, so they offered me the scholarship.

"Steve Smear had a lot to do with it. He kept sort of recommending me to Joe Paterno and George Welsh. But I was surprised when Penn State came after me. That was big-time football, the only big-time team to recruit me. If I had been sought after by five or six other major colleges, it would have been one thing. But to readjust your thinking from VMI to Penn State, it's a little bit of a shock.

"I don't even remember anything from the first conversation I had with Joe. It was more a casual interview, or a discussion. And George hadn't come down to Virginia to see me play. He had just seen a film of me. That's how casual the recruiting was. I think they just wanted to take a shot at someone. They had one scholarship left and they just took a shot at me."

Obviously Welsh had seen something he liked in that can of film, and so had Paterno. And Ham wasn't the first athlete to go from nobody to somebody. Ken Griffey lasted until the 29th round of baseball's free agent draft in 1969. Larry Bowa wasn't even drafted; in fact, he had been cut twice by his high school baseball coach. The Steelers won Super Bowls with players like offensive guard Sam David and safety Donnie Shell. The latter made All Pro; both had gone through the college player draft and were picked up by Pittsburgh as free agents.

The stunning thing about Ham's rise to stardom was that it happened so suddenly, even Jack wasn't prepared for it.

"I got up there after Penn State had turned itself around," he remembered. "They had an 8-2 season before I got up there and had gone to the Gator Bowl (in 1967). They played some quality teams and they had some great defensive players. Smear, Reid and John Ebersole were all playing for that football team.

"When I came to spring practice at the end of my freshman year, Paterno put me on the first team defense. I was out there with Reid and Smear and Ebersole and Dennis Onkotz and Jimmy Kates and Neal Smith. These guys were coming into their own as a great defensive unit and I was part of it. That really turned my career around.

"I was flabbergasted, in shock. They give you the shirts for whatever unit you are on, and they gave you a blue shirt if you were on the first team. All the guys on the freshman team were highly-recruited players but I found out early in my freshman year that I could play with those guys. But all of a sudden to be on the first team defense was really a shocker."

In the fall, Ham was joined by another sophomore, defensive back Mike Smith, on the first unit, but in spring ball his first year, he was the only blue-shirted member of the class of '71.

"I spent a week with Joe Paterno down in St. Thomas recently and I finally asked him why it happened," Ham said. "He explained there were some players who came along who were instinctive players. He said it wasn't a real big coaching decision on his part, that he had seen other players at Penn State who were natural players and instinctively good players. He said I was like them. He said it was without question that he did what he did when I was a freshman and that made me feel very good. I was puzzled as to why he did it at the time, but he said he couldn't take that much credit, that it wasn't that much of a coaching decision. He said it was something that stuck out to him and all of the coaches, that I was a player."

The rest of Lion Country found out quickly enough. His sophomore year, Ham specialized in blocked punts with three, two in extremely important situations. At UCLA, Jim Kates scooped up one of them and ran 36 yards for State's first touchdown in a game it would win, 21-6. Against Miami (Fla.), he blocked another deep in Hurricane territory and the Nittany Lions went in for their third touchdown in a come-from-behind 22-7 victory. He was fifth on the team in tackles as Penn State won all its games on the way to the epic Orange Bowl finish against Kansas. And the following year, he was second on the team in tackles and he blocked another punt as Penn State ran its winning streak to 22 in a row with an Orange Bowl victory over Missouri.

Ham played both those seasons carrying less than 200 pounds on his 6-3 frame. And the game he remembers most was the one that almost ruined the streak.

"The happiest moments had to be the Orange Bowl victories," Ham said, "but the one game I'll never forget was in 1969 at Syracuse. We always had trouble at Syracuse and this day we were losing, 14-0, early in the fourth quarter. We were playing horrible football, but Joe kept his poise on the sidelines, just like he did in the (1981) Pitt game. He said, 'Keep plugging away, something good is going to happen. Keep hustling and you'll be able to pull this one out.' His attitude was that a team is going to play great against you, and you just have to hang in there, be disciplined and don't get away from what you're doing. And darn if we don't recover a fumble and Franco (Harris) busts one for 40 yards and a touchdown. Then we get the ball right back and score and win it, 15-14. The way we played, we should have lost, but that game and the way Joe acted on the sidelines has had a great effect on me, not just at Penn State but right over into the pros.

"After we won our first Super Bowl with the Steelers, Chuck Noll would always tell us, 'Listen, every football team that we're going to play, New

A perennial NFL All-Pro player with the Pittsburgh Steelers, Jack Ham blitzes Bengal quarterback Ken Anderson.

Jack Ham has earned four diamond rings from the Super Bowl as a member of the Pittsburgh Steelers.

Orleans and all the way down the line, they're going to play their best football against you.' And it had been just like that at Penn State. For the first quarter or the first two quarters, a team would be sky-high. They weren't that great a team but they would play way over their heads because they wanted to knock off Penn State. "I think I was fortunate to play under Paterno. He taught me a lot more than just about winning football games."

In fact, in 1970, Joe Paterno taught his team how to lose with style. The 23-game streak came down against Colorado in the foothills of the Rockies. After the game, shocked Buffalo football players watched as Paterno entered their locker room with a smile on his face and patted Colorado coach Eddie Crowder on the back.

"How can he smile after what happened to him?" one player asked.

"That's why they win all the time," replied another. "They have class."

The Lions lost to Wisconsin and Syracuse in Ham's senior year before Paterno benched the two quarterbacks he had been alternating in favor of sophomore John Hufnagel.

"Senior year was a disappointment," Ham admitted. "But it was understandable. We had lost a lot of the defensive players. The two previous years, the defense had carried the football team and won a lot of games for it, but we just couldn't do that my senior year. Remember, in the Orange Bowl against Missouri, we had nine turnovers and scored ten points. You would think with nine turnovers that you would be scoring in the 40's. But the defense had to win that football game and that was as good a defensive effort as I've ever seen by a college football team. But we weren't able to withstand that kind of pressure my senior year and we just didn't have the horses on offense to make up for it."

The Nittany Lions might have lacked some horses that year, but Jack Ham was recognized as a thoroughbred. If no one had noticed him previous to the Colorado game, they picked up on him against the Buffalos when he made 15 unassisted tackles. But some of the pro scouts were skeptical. Those were the days when major barometers of whether or not a player was a prospect were a stopwatch and scale. Ham was able to conquer the stopwatch. The scale was his enemy. His senior year, the Penn State press guide listed him as 212 pounds. They must have weighed him with bricks in his pockets. He played at about 200 and wondered if he had the bulk to run with the pros.

"Initially, I didn't even know if I would play pro ball or not," he said. "I started getting some feelers from the pro teams, but I had the misconception that you had to be 250 pounds and bite peoples' heads off to be a linebacker in the NFL. But then before the draft, teams started to call me, saying, wouldn't you like to play for Los Angeles or whoever else.

"Right before the draft, I got a call from the Giants, so I thought I was going there. They indicated they were going to take me in the first round. So when I got drafted by the Steelers in the second round, I guess I was disappointed."

It wasn't, Ham explained, simply going from a winning program to a losing one (the Steelers had been 1-13 and 5-9 in Noll's first two years).

"I didn't want to be around here, because I had been in this area all my life, from Johnstown to Penn State. Now I wanted an opportunity to play somewhere else. Plus, I didn't think the Steeler defense was the right style for me. It was toe to toe. I liked the San Diego style better. So I was disappointed. Funny, isn't it? Things couldn't have turned out better."

After Ham's rookie year, the Steelers drafted another Penn Stater, Franco Harris. And the two Nittany Lions were very instrumental in turning the Steelers from losers to four-time Super Bowl champs. Through the mid and late 1970's, Ham was a regular for the AFC in the Pro Bowl. He is one of the all-time league leaders among linebackers in interceptions. He has four diamond rings from the Super Bowl and, in the off-season, he works with the stuff of which diamonds are made.

He is a salesman for the Neville Coal Co., in Pittsburgh. Two decades ago, you might have felt sorry for him, getting involved in a dying industry. But now coal sales are thriving.

"About four or five years ago, I was playing racquet ball in the off-season and I met the man who owns our company," Ham said. "He told me, 'We're starting a coal company and if you like us and we like you, it might be a good venture.' And it's worked out very well. "The price of coal in 1974 (because of the Arab oil embargo) went right through the roof. Now it's leveling off. Right now, our biggest business is in the international market. Poland was a big exporter of coal but when they stopped production, the other European countries had to find another source, which they did by coming to the Eastern United States. And we have plenty of it. There's enough coal here for the next several hundred years.

"My job is selling coal to domestic utilities. Most of our business is in the Ohio and Michigan areas. The situation with foreign oil has put us in a position where most utilities have converted from oil to coal. So I think coal is here to stay."

The big question now is how long Jack Ham will stay in professional football. It's one he can't answer.

"I'm going to take it a year at a time," he says. "It depends on how I feel physically. I make that decision when the season is over. If I get banged up a lot, I'm sure that will be a major factor, but I feel pretty good right now and I enjoy playing. It's still a lot of fun, but once that changes, I'll get out of the game."

And probably into the coal business fulltime. In a way, it seems only fitting because it's not that many years ago that Ham was a high school senior sitting on the bench at Bishop McCort, wondering if he would ever be noticed.

A diamond in the rough, you might say.

Scott Fitzkee celebrates game-winning touchdown catch at North Carolina State in 1977.

10
SCOTT FITZKEE

If Jack Ham was America's best kept football secret at the end of his high school career, Scott Fitzkee was a rumor that spread like crabgrass. Terrific athlete over there in Pennsylvania Dutch country. Not very heavy in the weight department. Extremely heavy in the statistics department.

"My sport in high school was probably football, but even that's hard to say," Fitzkee admitted from his San Diego apartment. "I think in my three years of football, I averaged something like 10.8 yards a carry. And I did pretty well in two other sports. I averaged about 21 points a game over three years in basketball, and in track I only lost about two races, not counting the state track meet. I ran a 9.6 (for 100 yards) two or three times and I ran a bunch of 9.7s."

So the recruiters came from all over, promising all kinds of on-the-field rewards. Scott Fitzkee listened to them all and in the end chose Penn State.

One of the reasons was that the Nittany Lions told him that he might not start until he was a junior.

Another was that they told him he would be switched from running back to wide receiver or perhaps defensive back.

Most recruits don't want to hear things like that. They want to be told that they will start every game in their college careers, that they will—All-America players by the time they are juniors and—by the way—the university has already ordered the plane tickets to New York City for when they accept the Heisman Trophy after their senior season.

The kid's eyes light up when he hears all of it and he signs on the dotted line. And more times than not, winds up with a career dotted with mediocrity. After four years, he spends his Sunday afternoons watching the National Football League on television instead of playing in it.

The Fitzkee family, though, had been prepared. For one thing, Scott's father had been the head coach at Red Lion for many years until he gave up football to become the high school principal at Red Lion High School when Scott was in seventh grade. For another, the family had heard all the insincere babble when older brother Ron, a linebacker, was heavily recruited two years earlier. Fool me once, shame on you. Fool me twice, shame on me!

"My brother had originally gone to the University of Virginia, so I thought about going there," Fitzkee remembered. I thought Maryland, I thought Villanova, I thought Syracuse. I went down to Texas Christian for a visit and I really liked it down there, so I guess I had six schools in my mind. I had been thinking about those places and then I made my decision in about a second. I said to myself, 'Hey, I'm going to Penn State. Why would I want to go anyplace else?'

"I visited a lot of schools and a lot of people said a lot of bad things. Things like that I would start right away. I was a running back in high school and they would say, 'You can start for us right away as a running back.' Well, I was 160 or 165 pounds at the time and my thoughts were, 'Are you crazy?' But at Penn State they told me that I would most likely be a wide receiver or maybe even a defensive back and they said things like, 'You might not play until maybe you're a junior.'

"I realize a lot of people that age can get caught up in it all, but I was lucky in that I had a brother who had just gone through it all and that helped a lot. You see, he went down to Virginia under one coach, but when he got there, another coach was there."

The other coach was Ulmo (Sonny) Randle, Virginia alumnus and former great NFL wide receiver. Virginia was starving for a winning football program and Randle promised them one. Instead, he gave them a near mutiny. In two years, the program went from 4-7 to 1-10.

"The year my brother left Virginia, 52 players left the team," Fitzkee remembered. "It was just real bad, you know, lying to him, getting people up at six in the morning if they had been late for a meeting or missed some practice time, things like that. But he had gone through the whole recruiting thing before me. I was around and heard and saw, so that was a big help to me.

"When Ron went to Virginia, I think the coach's name was Don Lawrence and he was pretty good. We all liked him. But then Sonny Randle got there and that immediately changed things around."

And by the time Scott Fitzkee entered the recruiting wars, Penn State had changed things around. The Nittany Lions were now recognized as a legitimate national power. In the mid-1950's, only the Harrisburg paper offered out-of-town coverage. Now all the Philadelphia and Pittsburgh papers, plus the New York Times and Long Island Newsday, were regularly staffing Joe Paterno's team.

But, Fitzkee said, all of that had nothing to do with his decision to enroll at State. Nor was there a lifelong ambition to play for his home state university.

"I hadn't even followed Penn State a whole lot when I was younger," he said. "Why, I don't know, but Joe Paterno's presence didn't have a lot to do with my decision. Getting to know his honesty and getting to know him had a lot to do with it, but there was no initial shock of, 'Hey, Joe Paterno, the head coach, he's at my house!' But getting to know the kind of man he was had a lot to do with my decision."

By that time, Fitzkee had already gotten to know an athlete one year his senior from Pittston, Pa. They had run against each other several times. The other athlete had also decided to attend Penn State. His name was Jimmy Cefalo.

"The first time I ever met Jimmy, we both ran in the Junior Olympics and we were both pretty young, about 13 or 14," Fitzkee said. "I remember we ran against each other at Franklin Field once. We ran against each other in the state track meet up at Penn State. And I beat him every time I raced him."

Fitzkee and Cefalo would bump heads in college, too. Scott's sophomore year, he and Jimmy shared the flanker spot, one of the few downers in Fitzkee's four years in college. And in the drive toward Super Bowl XVI that neither player achieved, Scott and Jimmy were on opposite sides of the field for the NFL's greatest game ever—the San Diego-Miami playoff.

By the time both players reached Lion Country, they were no longer sprinter-swift. Each had begun to bulk up a bit for the challenge of major college football. Scott quickly gained 10 to 15 pounds, then quickly gave a demonstration of his potential in the third game of his freshman season against Ohio State.

By this time, Paterno was mellowing in his former militant stand against the NCAA legislation that allowed freshmen to compete at the varsity level. The change had been gradual; to this day, Paterno will not allow the name of a freshman recruit in the Nittany Lion press guide.

However, when he found himself short of tailbacks before the 1972 game against Illinois, he took along first-year man Woody Petchel as a precautionary measure. By 1974, Cefalo and tight end Randy Sidler were taking regular shifts with the offense. And by 1975, reporters who covered Penn State regularly were used to shouting, "Who's he, where's he from," when some freshman would do something out of the ordinary.

On the day of the Ohio State game in 1975, the answers would be, "Scott Fitzkee, Red Lion, Pa."

John Andress was the quarterback when Fitzkee sneaked into the lineup early in the second half before the normal capacity crowd at Ohio Stadium.

Scott ran a fly pattern down the right sideline and Andress threw the ball towards him. The pass was overthrown but the Nittany Lion from Red Lion stretched as far as he could and made a sensational diving catch.

"That was my first college highlight," Fitzkee said. "Another, of course, was playing·on a team that got a chance to play for the national championship. But in between there was a low point."

Fitzkee had come out of spring ball his freshman year listed as the number one split end. He had caught only one more pass during his freshman season but appeared to have a regular spot for his sophomore season.

"I went home for the summer and came back to State expecting to be the split end," he said. "But when pre-season practice began, I was a backup on the other side and I ended up alternating at flanker with Jimmy Cefalo. Now I'm not trying to take anything away from Jimmy. He's a great player. But that was a real downer for me because I didn't feel there was any reason I shouldn't have been the starter (Tom Donovan and Rich Mauti wound up alternating at split end). I asked for reasons many times and got answers like, 'Well, you didn't have a good week of practice,' things like that which I considered ridiculous.

"Some games, I would alternate a lot and some games I would hardly play. I might be put in for a running down and, on a passing situation, someone else would come in. The reason for that was that I was the punter and they might have wanted to rest me on third down. But, first of all, if I weren't in, I'd get down on myself and, as a result, I might not punt the ball as well as I could. I'd be down on myself and down on them for not having me in there. I felt I could run a long route and still be in good enough condition that my leg would probably be looser and I might be able to punt the ball better.

"And then we got to the Gator Bowl, against Notre Dame, and I hardly played at all. That was the lowest point of my college career."

Happiness for Scott Fitzkee is a touchdown catch before the home folks at Beaver Stadium. (opposite page)

The rest was an ascending high until the final game in the Superdome. As a junior, Fitzkee was switched back to split end, where he started every game. One of them was at North Carolina State.

For some reason or another, the Wolfpack have a history of giving Penn State fits. This particular season, the reason was a stocky dynamo named Ted Brown, who carried the ball 37 times for 251 maddening yards. With less than three minutes left, Penn State had the ball on its own 17, trailing by 17-14. Chuck Fusina, who was to establish school records for pass completions (22) and passing yardage (315), quickly marched the team down the field, hitting Cefalo with three passes and tight end Mickey Shuler with two more. Now the ball was on the Wolfpack 11. Fusina called a play in the huddle, didn't like what he saw at the line of scrimmage and changed his mind.

"He called out to me at the last moment and changed the call," Fitzkee remembered, "I caught the ball and we won the game."

True to his theory, Fitzkee played almost every down as a junior and improved his punting average from 35.4 to 38.6 yards. His senior year, his average slipped back to 34.6 but 11 of his 65 punts dropped inside the 20 yard line and the total return yardage against him was a puny 84. In contrast Penn State returned 98 opponents' punts for a total of 591 yards.

And those were the kind of statistics that framed the perfect regular season. Ohio State coach started freshman quarterback Art Schlichter; the Penn State defense beat on him mercilessly. Fusina marched the offense up and down the field, passing to Fitzkee or handing off to future pros Matt Suhey, Booker Moore, Mike Guman and Bob Torrey. Keith Dorney, Irv Pankey, Eric Cunningham and Chuck Correal—future pros all—were the main offensive linemen. A couple of sophomore backups, Mike Munchak and Sean Farrell, were first round choices in the 1982 pro draft.

The two most obvious rocks on the defense were tackles Matt Millen and Brice Clark. Matt Bahr handled the placekicking. In all, 26 players who made the trip to the Sugar Bowl to play Alabama would later play in the pros, an awesome statistic.

And yet Penn State got off to a horrible start in the Superdome, fell less than a yard short of a chance for victory or a tie late in the fourth quarter, then saw their program turn full cycle from what had happened that day a decade before.

On January 1, 1969, Penn State got its chance to win its first major bowl game of the Joe Paterno Era when Kansas had 12 men on the field.

On January 1, 1979, Penn State blew its chance to win its first national championship because it had 12 men on the field in a critical situation.

"I remember a lot of opportunities we had and that we didn't capitalize on them," Fitzkee said. "The big thing was that Barry Krauss stopped us down at the goal line (after Fitzkee had caught a pass inside the one, setting up third-and-goal). He stopped Matt (Suhey) and Mike (Guman). But I still don't

Scott Fitzkee, then with Eagles, celebrates a touchdown catch against Denver Broncos in 1980 opener.

think we lost that game. I think it was more that we gave it away. After Krauss stopped us, they shanked a punt out of the end zone to the 20 yard line but we had 12 men on the field. There were so many opportunities we had and blew. Maybe it wouldn't have made a difference, but I still think we should have beaten them by a touchdown or two. But it was exciting. And not many people get a chance to play for the national championship."

And, if Fitzkee's on-the-field experiences at Penn State were mostly great, his off-the-field experiences were all super. And part of that was the presence of Joe Paterno.

"I'm sure you could call him a disciplinarian," Fitzkee said. "Little things, like you'd be one minute late for a meeting, and he'd be all over you. Miss class and you'd be in trouble. A bad grade would get you in trouble. But that was fine, because Joe was trying to make a whole person out of you, not just a football player. I mean, how many people are going to get a chance to play pro ball? Ninety-five percent of the guys are going to have to go out in the real world and find out what it's all about.

"I learned an awful lot from Joe, so I don't think I'll have any trouble when my football career is over being a businessman or whatever it is that I eventually do. Coming out of Joe's program, I have to think that I've got an edge over players coming out of other programs. By his making a person out of you, you learn a lot about different things beside football."

Fitzkee believes that Paterno, who has turned down several NFL offers, would make a good pro coach.

"I'm sure of it, because he adapts to any situation and he's obviously a very intelligent person," he said. "I don't think he would use his college routine in the pros. In the pros, you have to discipline to a certain extent, but we're also talking about 35-year-old men who have 15-year-old sons at home."

But, then again, maybe Paterno wouldn't have to change his routine. After all, Fitzkee's first professional coach never changed his.

Fitzkee was drafted by the Philadelphia Eagles in the fifth round. He knew that fact alone would make him borderline. And he knew he had to impress. Instead he pressed. The head coach was Dick Vermeil, a man who is long on coaching ability and short on patience. Also, all college rah-rah, straight from UCLA and the Rose Bowl to Philadelphia and, eventually, the Super Bowl.

"I played for him for more than two years," Fitzkee said, "and I still don't know how he does it. I think he just scares everybody into working. I know I was running scared from him from day one. And now I'm playing for some-one (Don Coryell) who is entirely the opposite.

"Playing for Vermeil was a real experience, I'll tell you. I went down there not knowing if I had a chance to make the team or not. I went down there a month early, but I started out real slow and, right down to the wire, I didn't know if I was going to make it. Confidence is so important a part of the game and I didn't have a lot of it at that point. Every rookie, I think, goes in there scared. I survived the final cut and you wouldn't believe how much I improved in the next few days. It's all a part of that confidence factor. Now I was able to go out there feeling like a professional athlete. In one week's time I was a different player."

Fitzkee played sparingly for the Eagles in 1979, but went into the 1980 season with renewed excitement because of a conversation he had with Vermeil in the weight room in the off-season.

"If you don't play for him, you never find out the kind of man he really is," Scott said. "All you hear about him is that he's a workaholic, that he works 19 hours a day, that he's a crazy man on the field. Well, after my rookie year, we were both working out. We were the only two people in the weight room. You know what an emotional guy he is. He gets choked up a little and he tells me that he thinks I have a pretty good opportunity to beat Charlie (Smith, a starting wide receiver) out that year. And after he got that out of the way, we talked for about 40 minutes. We talked about my family, about my brother, about everything but football. It was really neat, seeing the other side of a head coach. We talked about everything from the President on down."

Vermeil was right about Fitzkee's chances of beating out Smith. They actually finished dead even and were alternating at the position until Fitzkee went down with a broken foot in the fourth game. He reinjured the foot in the NFC playoff semi-final against Minnesota, sat out part of the 1981 season while waiting for the full mend, then was grabbed off the waiver wire by the Chargers before the 12th week of the season. And now the Charger people are hinting that they hope he will eventually replace the aging Charlie Joiner. And most people who know him figure he will eventually become a success in something other than football.

And Scott Fitzkee will credit a lot of whatever future success he does enjoy to his days in Lion Country.

"One reason I went up there was that they had no athletic dorms," he said. "We had to live in the regular dorms for three years and the dorms I lived in had maybe four other football players, so I got to know a lot of guys who were just regular students.

"A lot of people ask me, 'Is it really true, all that stuff about Paterno's Grand Experiment,' and I tell them it is. I think in your college days, you can learn as much—if not more—from your social life than from what you learn in the classroom. You go out in life for the first time and you meet people from all over. For me, the whole thing was a terrific experience."

Mike Reid played defensive tackle for Penn State and in 1969 was the Nittany Lions first unanimous All-America choice. In addition, Mike won both the Outland Trophy and the Maxwell Trophy in 1969.

11
MIKE REID

Joe Paterno called it "The Grand Experiment."

"We want our players to enjoy football," he said in the late 1960's when the Nittany Lions were winning every autumn Saturday. "We want them to enjoy college. We want them to learn about art and literature and music and all the other things college has to offer. It's the only time a person is really free. We don't want them just tied to a football program."

He surrounded himself with good examples. Neal Smith, the walk-on who became an All-America safety and a civil engineering major. Dennis Onkotz, the All-America linebacker who used to go to class on Saturday mornings before games to earn credits toward his major, biophysics. Gary Gray, the electrical engineering major who kept switching jobs after graduation because his fertile mind became bored after mastering each one.

Nearly all the Penn State football players earned their degree, a cause of much national celebration. But one player was special. How many football players (1) are credited with two safeties in their first college game, (2) play the organ at church during college, (3) appear on the Tonight Show with Johnny Carson as something other than a football player, (4) make All-America in college and All Pro in the NFL, then turn their backs on the sport at the prime of their career, (5) are equally comfortable listening to Bach, the Beatles and Barbara Mandrell and (6) can honestly say their biggest thrill was hearing someone sing a song they had written?

Mike Reid can say yes to all six of those statements. He can also tell you that he lives for that one great moment of drama in any situation, that he found it once at Penn State, that he never found it in his five years with the

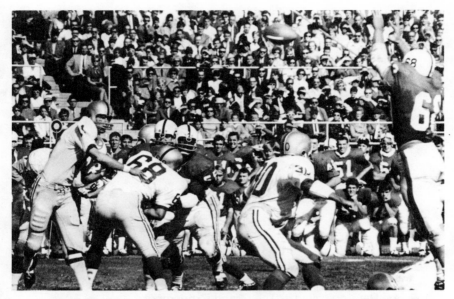

Mike Reid gets set to bat down pass by the West Virginia quarterback in 1969.

Mike Reid, studying in college for his ultimate vocation—sharps and flats, not Xs and Os.

Cincinnati Bengals and that he is now finding it in Nashville, Tenn. And that the theory that some people have formulated about him—that all his life he believed he was a musician who happened to play football while the rest of the world thought him a football player who happened to play music—wasn't true at all.

"The truth is that it took me a long, long time to think of myself as a musician," Reid said. "I don't think you can be in an environment that is as emotionally dynamic as football and have a bit of notoriety as we did at Penn State and then have success in the NFL, with all of that you cannot then stand up and declare, 'No, this isn't really me. I'm someone else.'

"I didn't mind the fact that I was a football player. And I got into the game for a particular reason. I mean, athletes do get into athletics for a particular reason. Without getting into the amateur psychology of it, you get into it because it seems like a fun thing to do. That's why I started playing football in the sandlots of Altoona. It was because it was fun. I was probably seven or eight when I started playing football in the neighborhood. I lived in a good neighborhood with a lot of kids and we were always doing one thing or another. If it wasn't specifically football, it was probably something that inadvertently related to the game. My brothers and I had a physical childhood.

"I started piano when I was six. I don't particularly know why. My mother and dad were not the kind of people who forced their kids into doing something like that. I asked to take lessons. My grandmother next door had an upright piano. I must have heard something, or maybe it was something in school. I don't know."

Piano was fun, just like football. And eventually both became sources of income, visible means of support. And yet Reid was never overly concerned about money. His excitement was generated by that high moment of drama. Great moments on the music scale were far more important than great numbers on the salary scale. And the highest football drama in Reid's career was reached with Miami's Orange Bowl providing the backdrop. The year was 1969. Among the other principal players on the stage were Neal Smith, Bobby Campbell and Chuck Burkhart.

It was the 15-14 victory over Kansas in which Reid helped give the Lions a chance for the win by sacking Bobby Douglass twice in the last two minutes.

"That game is probably my fondest moment of anything I've ever done in sports, before or since," he said. "The first sack was a rollout as I recall, and the second was a dropback. I think when I did it at the time, I didn't particularly think it would come to anything because it looked pretty much like we were going to lose. And I think as an athlete I was pretty much of a realist all my life. I was never the kind of athlete you could tell to run through a brick wall and I would do it with blind obedience."

A lot of people across America remember a scene on television at about that stage of the game. They recall a TV camera isolating on Reid and the announcer pointing out that Mike was deep in prayer, eyes closed, hands folded. The scene was deeply touching. Also deeply false.

"It's an example of the power of the image the media—in this case TV—can create," Reid said. "What really happened was that I was sitting on the bench and, of course, it was extremely hot. I think that was when the Hong Kong Flu was going around and I went into that game with a bit of that flu. The heat was to my advantage because I was able to sweat a lot of that junk out of me. But we had come to that critical moment of the game and, as I recall, there was a picture taken that made it appear that I was praying.

"What happened was that I had just wiped the sweat off my head and my face. My hands had been brought down to my chin and my eyes were closed. So it probably appeared that I was praying, but I don't recall that I really was. I don't think the big play had taken place. I was just wiping the sweat off my face at the time the TV camera came on and someone said, 'Isn't that touching and moving' and whatever. I was sitting on the bench because I was never one to stand up and watch the game when I wasn't in it. It was enough for me to be on the field. I liked to rest in between."

So Reid was sitting on the bench when the Burkhart-to-Campbell miracle occurred and the American Broadcasting Company had its prayer answered. And Mike Reid didn't even see his moment of drama, his football version of the segment in the 1812 Overture where the cannons boom and the bells chime. And, hard as it may seem to believe, the 1969 Orange Bowl scene was the last to thrill Reid even though he would be a unanimous All-America pick the following year, would finish high for a defensive lineman in the Heisman Trophy voting and would be an All-Pro.

In other words, he doesn't even have any vivid memories of the 1970 Orange Bowl in which he captained a defensive unit that put on one of the great shows in history?

"No, and I'll tell you why," Reid said. "I think for me that 1969 win over Kansas climaxed an awfully 'fun' year, an enjoyable year of football for a young kid to live through in college. It was particular fun for me because I had come off that knee operation and that year as a redshirt and I think if Joe Paterno or anyone else had said they were sure I'd be coming back off that, they'd have been telling a little white lie.

"For one thing, it was my second knee problem. My first operation was in high school. And I'm relatively sure it was believed that I would never play again because somehow I remember being asked to go to Jacksonville for the 1967 Gator Bowl game. Christmastime for me has always been a special time like it is for most people, so I don't remember specifically wanting to go to that game. But I ended up going by way of train with the band.

"The arrangement was that I would fly back with team. But I was informed after the game that there were no seats left. The message was there: 'We'll see ya, Mike, when we see ya.' I specifically remember Richie Lucas' sentence to me was 'I don't know what to tell you, Mike.'

"There was a guy who played at Penn State some years before me named Chuck Gillard and we somehow got a flight out of there, thanks to a guy named Galen Dreibelbis, who was a real supporter of Penn State. He turned out to be a good friend of Penn State over the years. Galen loaned me his credit card so I could rent a car in Pittsburgh. I drove home in a snowstorm. But if it hadn't been for Galen Dreibelbis, I might still be in Jacksonville.

"The distinct feeling I had back then was, 'Kid, it's over with.' I had the feeling that I would probably never play again. And I guess the reason for remembering that story was that it made my return year all the more meaningful. And then senior year the win streak continued, but I'll tell you, I don't remember much enjoyment out of my senior year at all. In fact, the thing I remember most about my senior year was when we went up to Syracuse and they beat the crap out of us. And those Syracuse guys deserved so much to win that game that I almost felt guilty. I remember thinking after that game, 'If we haven't lost this one, it's unlikely that we even know how to lose,' because they had just beaten us ten ways to hell and back. I know I got killed, and I know most everybody else did on defense. Of course in those days, we had all the wins and we were the unconquerables, so you would never come out and publically admit that you had gotten soundly pounded into the ground.

"I remember coming back from the 1969 Orange Bowl and being met by all the students and my feeling so proud of us and all of us being so proud to be at that school and happy to be on that team and happy to be part of that whole deal, so the 11 games that remained in my college career were fairly anti-climactic.

"I don't really remember anything about that second Orange Bowl game other than our inability to score. I think it was probably a stinking game for the country to watch. But I think you also have to remember that the Kansas game was a dull game, too, up to the last two minutes.

"My most fond Penn State athletic memories, other than the first Orange Bowl, were throwing the shot put on the track team", (with no prior experience, Reid broke the Penn State record during the first meet, then broke his own record twice) "and working with Bill Cole on the wrestling team" (where he advanced as a heavyweight deep into the NCAA tournament before being defeated by eventual champ Granville Liggons).

The writers who covered Reid had their own fond memories of the guy with the ability to make several spectacular plays per Saturday. His quotes were thoughtful and original and often humorous.

Informed that he had failed to win the Heisman Trophy: "I don't even know who Heisman was. For all I know, he might have been a falling-down drunk in Albuquerque."

Getting his turn to accept a Maxwell Club Award after hearing a series of high school players credit their coaches and parents before profusely thanking the club: "Gentlemen, I did it all by myself and to hell with you."

Explaining his quickness in getting off the line of scrimmage: "Quickness is merely a muscular response to any given stimulus."

On his musical skills: "I know I look a lot more like a piano mover than a piano player."

On a dislocated finger that he popped back into place on the field during his first college game: "I looked down at my finger. It had been rendered concave."

He could create a story, then recreate it better than anyone. And now he was moving on, the seventh selection overall in the NFL and the first pick of the Cincinnati Bengals.

"I'm not an idealist, but in all my athletic career, I never asked for anything in return other than what I put out," he said. "In a sense, to be an athlete was its own reward. I never asked for a lot of money. I never equated athletic performance with x-amount of dollars. And I don't have any specific memories of really wanting to be a pro football player. I probably just wanted to see if I could do it. There was the challenge and the curiosity.

"I was never in my life someone who was a pure athlete, who did it just for athletic reasons. I think it was more of a case of my always searching for the dramatic aspect. The idea of winning and losing was always secondary to the dramatic implications of the game, spoken in a universal that transcends language."

Like, perhaps, the last play of the first half of the 1981 San Diego-Miami playoff game?

"Exactly!" Reid bellowed. "What a great example. That was Shula's genius. And that's what the sport was about for me. It was also in Bobby Campbell's catch in the last minutes. Charlie Burkhart, who was very much an average-to-fair passer, pulling that off, that's what the game is about. I suppose you always played subconsciously as an athlete, looking for those few moments like that, something to really latch on to."

They are moments that never came in the professional career of one Michael Reid.

"I got a call from the Bengals the day I was drafted and two days later I flew into Cincinnati to meet Paul Brown," Reid said. "He was a terribly disarming man. He was a wonderful man to walk into an office and meet. I was immediately glad that I was going to get to play for him.

"You'd be amazed to know what I, as a first round draft pick, was paid. My base salary was $22,000. I had a good season for them, made Rookie of the

Year and they gave me an enormous raise—to $35,000 or $40,000. I didn't know what I was worth, and I had no sense about what the market value of an athlete was. But if you are getting into athletics, or music for that matter, simply to make a lot of money, that is not the right reason to be doing it. That kind of thinking can consume you. I really think it's an energy proposition and you better be committed enough to put all your energies into doing that one thing.

"Throughout the five years I played for them, whenever I produced they tore up my contract and gave me a new one without my asking. I never had any money qualms. I love the system by which we live in this country and I'm not against money. It's just that it's an absolute monstrous waste of energy to have that thought consume your life. And I was real lucky in my life to be involved in something like sports where I realized if I tended to my store...the financial end would take care of itself.

"My rookie year was a lot of fun, to discover that I could play and be competitive in the NFL. I remember in the exhibition season we played Cleveland and there I was, face to face with Gene Hickerson who was a perennial All-Pro. Fortunately I got Gene at the end of his career. I wouldn't have wanted to play him in his prime.

"In the playoffs we played Baltimore and there I was, tackling Johnny Unitas. My rookie year was the Bengals' third season and the town was having fun with its new team. We didn't always win but we gave the people a good show. We were a bunch of young kids who played with a lot of enthusiasm and we were a lot of fun to watch. And then came a couple of awards that told me I could compete in the league. But I don't remember a particularly enjoyable season after that. From then on, it was the same speeches, the same everything. The same playbook. In my five years, I found out there was very little creativity in football and I think that had to bother anybody that had any kind of thought level that rises above the size of his helmet or grass drills. It has to bother anyone who thinks anything at all about other aspects of life."

Is it the same lack of creativity that engulfs, perhaps, a worker on an automobile assembly line?

"Yes, but that is not to equate the two, because theirs on the assembly line is tenfold," Reid said. "But I know what you're saying. In one sense, the head comes around and bites the tail, in that you are so well cared for. You get to stay in the best hotels, you eat the best food, you travel first class. You don't have to do anything, you don't have to think. Just come. You are told where to come and at what time. This is what you wear to do what you do. This bus is leaving, you be on this bus. This is what you eat, we're all going to eat together. If we go to a movie, we all go to the same movie. It's the same playbook, the same this and the same that. And I guess for anyone who got into

Now that he's writing songs instead of chasing quarterbacks, Mike Reid can offer a laid-back, 50-pound-lighter look.

the game for those moments of drama, for someone who required that to be fulfilled, it was just a slow death situation.

"Drudgery is very much the right word and it becomes that from the very first time you ask yourself, 'Why am I doing this?' I'll tell you a phrase that makes me cringe when I hear an athlete say it—'Well, that's my job.' I don't think a job is what sports is about. Unfortunately, maybe it has become that. And why is it a job now? Because it's become such a ponderous business situation.

"I was beginning to feel when I was in the league that the real story of sports is not about winning. It's not about victory over insurmountable odds. It's not about trial and triumph. It's about coping with failure more than it is about winning.

"It's for example, the Super Bowl this year. The Bengals came out of nowhere and pull off this miraculous year and suddenly you had people in Cincinnati who weren't sure if the football was the long one or the round one or whether it was blown up or stuffed talking about 'my team', like they had been down there through it all. They came out of the woodwork, which was great because it gave the guys on the Bengals their moment in the sun after a long, ugly, ugly, ugly situation in that town. And there's nothing that can bring out ugliness in a town than a losing sports franchise.

"And now they have this miraculous year, but they lose in the Super Bowl. And now there's nothing about what a wonderful year they had. The city has dropped the team momentarily like a hot potato. It's the tragedy of the loss.

"You know, I often think about Fran Tarkenton and those other Minnesota guys. They are never thought of as a team that went to the Super Bowl four times. They were the ones who lost four times.

"Things turn around so quickly. Look at the situation in Pittsburgh. It's beyond me how the real football fan in that city could turn his back on that football team just because those guys got old and started losing."

Yet Reid turned his back on the sport in the prime years of his career. An explanation?

"I was just a young guy who happened to be physically large and was able to maneuver my size around with some grace," he explained. "It was never a religion for me. But in sports there seems to be that residue. The last page of so many sports stories is coping with failure rather than reflecting on any great moments in the sun. Look at Ali. And Frazier. They try to come back and they're fat, not in shape. It's heartbreaking, really. As for me, you hear this phrase a lot in the psychological-babble circles—job burnout. I might have had it left physically, but mentally I was burned out. My last year in the league, I remember getting moments of such depression about what I was doing that I could really feel it starting to physically impair me. And I realized that I was so young—only 27 at the time. I thought to myself, 'This is a shame, to dissipate all this young energy doing something that you don't want to do anymore."

To have that part of your conscience screeching at you is one thing. To have something else blaring at you through an insensitive management bullhorn is something else. Mike Reid's last year in the pros was the year of the first player strike. The owners allowed the camps to remain open. Free agents were trucked in like vegetables, and some of the IQ's matched the simile.

"One of the important things in an athlete's life is how he relates to his teammates," Reid said. "It's a weird kind of friendship you have at that level because there's a competitive edge on everything you do. There's a certain —I hate this word but I'll use it for lack of a better one—comraderie there. And yet there is a competitive edge that exists not only on the field during a game but in the locker room as well. 'This guy's bigger. This guy's faster. He's stronger. He's better. He starts, I don't start. He's smarter. He's not smart.' There's always that underlying theme there. And what you have there is a group of young, macho guys trying to measure up to some fuzzy, amorphous image of what the Great American Male is supposed to be.

"It's funny because athletes in most cases are a mass of contradictions. There **is** that feeling of living up to that (macho) image all the time, even among yourselves as a team. And yet there are a million things trying to get out as well—other kinds of emotions. Athletes, especially if they are professionals, can buy their way out of a lot of life's hassles. But there are other aspects of life that you just can't turn your back on. How other people look at you. How they relate to you. They laugh at you. You're a football player, so you must be stupid, that sort of thing. It's trite, but it still causes a certain amount of emotional discomfort.

"But, throughout it all, there's always that friendship that exists among teammates. And, in 1974, there was the strike. Some went into camp, some didn't go into camp, and it caused a lot of hatred among people you were going to play along side of. It was a big mistake on Paul Brown's part, keeping that camp open. Any franchise that kept its camp open during the strike made a big mistake. It drove a wedge right through the teams.

"And I don't know where the hell we learn. I don't specifically remember why we went to that Orange Bowl instead of the Cotton Bowl in 1970. On the surface, if you take tab A and fit it into slot B, it will tell you that we went to the Orange Bowl because the team voted on it and that's where we wanted to go. And that's crap. I don't really believe that Joe, or any alumni group or whoever runs the show would ever let a bunch of 18, 19, 20 year old kids cheat the university out of money.

"The only reason we were allowed to vote and we went to the Orange Bowl is because it was economically feasible to do so, because in anybody's right mind we should have gone to Dallas to play Texas. But I don't remember it being a particularly important thing at the time, but I do know that in the 13 years since it happened, I've occasionally thought about it. Not when I was playing pro football but just since I've gotten out. Certain things will trip my memory about when I played."

When the football died after the 1974 season, the musical dream lived on. Reid formed a band, then did a solo act. Eventually, he cut a demo that was sent to Nashville. One thing led to another and Reid was offered a writing position with a publishing house. And, by the spring of 1982, Reid found out that three of the songs he had written would be included in Ronnie Milsap's next album. He is working in Old Opry City, writing for a singer who is recognized as a country-western talent, yet Reid says he doesn't really know what C&W is. And he says that his transition from classical to rock to the borders of country isn't really a contradiction at all.

"I don't think it's a matter of whether it's country music or it's pop music or it's rock or it's Broadway or jazz," he says. "It's kind of a cliche, but I think the thing you look for in any kind of music is that one spark, that one element in a piece of music that really excites people. You can put any kind of label on it you want—soul, heart-and-soul, whether it's in the lyric or the melody or in the way the singer sings it. You can talk all you want about the soul in blues, but there's no one singing today that is any more soulful than, say, Merle Haggard or George Jones, both of whom are hard-core traditional country singers.

"Merle Haggard is a great singer. Milsap is the same way, but Milsap has a bit of a problem in that the guy is so amazingly talented that he can literally sing anything. And thus it is difficult for him to channel his energies in one direction.

"You know, there's lousy jazz and there's wonderful jazz. There's lousy country music and wonderful country music. There's terrible pop music and wonderful pop music. When you distill all the junk away, if you took the best of songs of every category, you would be hard-pressed to find someone who loved music that didn't find good, moving aspects in each type of song.

"And classical music! You tend to think that because people don't understand classical music, that they must think it all is good. Well, there's an awful lot of lousy, stinking classical music."

And now Reid finds himself with the new challenge. He never quite made number one on the charts at Penn State or with the Bengals, but he now seeks to write good music that will reach the top.

"I'm real lucky, I'll tell you," Reid says. "I'm one of the most fortunate people in the world to have done one thing, to have experienced the power of being in the athletic environment, and then turn around here at age 34 to become involved in something with more passion than ever before. To suddenly have those dreams again, real dreams beginning to come true. Things to be pointing toward, not goals but things that kind of draw you along in a good progressive direction. And I recently experienced a situation like that. Nothing I ever did as an athlete ever excited me or moved me as much as the first time I heard Ronnie Milsap sing one of my songs. I was in the studio the day it happened. To have gone through what I have gone through and then to be afforded this luxury is pretty fortunate.

"I think there's a critical problem with an athlete. There's no real way to prepare an athlete for the time he's going to stop playing. You become a junkie for one aspect of the game, which is not the physical aspect. It's being watched by 60,000 people, or, in some cases, several million on TV. You become a junkie for being noticed for doing something well. When that stops, if you don't have anything to transfer that addiction to, it can be emotionally devastating. Some guys never get out from underneath that.

"I knew I was ready to retire. One more year and they would have hauled me off to Fantasy Island permanently, but I still had to weigh it against the fact that this thing I was leaving was something I had done extremely well and that I would probably never do anything else in my life as well as it."

But that may not be a safe bet. Even within himself, Reid feels he is blossoming as a songwriter. He may truly be on his way to a second brilliant career.

For Mike Reid, the experiment called life has been truly grand.

A
HISTORY of GREATNESS

PENN STATE FOOTBALL ALL-TIME RESULTS

1887
54	at Bucknell	0
24	Bucknell	0
	(2-0)	

1888
6	Dickinson	6
0	at Dickinson	16
0	Lehigh	30
	(0-2-1)	

1889
20	Swarthmore	6
0	at Lafayette	26
0	at Lehigh	106
12	Bucknell	0
	(2-2)	

1890
0	at Penn	20
0	at Franklin and Marshall	10
68	Altoona	0
23	at Bellefonte	0
	(2-2)	

1891
14	at Lafayette	4
2	at Lehigh	24
44	at Swarthmore	0
26	at Franklin and Marshall	6
18	at Gettysburg	0
10	at Bucknell	12
2	Dickinson (forfeit)	0
58	at Haverford	0
	(6-2)	

1892
G. W. Hoskins, Coach
0	at Penn	20
44	Wyoming Seminary	0
16	Pittsburgh A. C.	0
18	Bucknell	0
18	Lafayette (Wilkes-Barre)	0
16	Dickinson (Harrisburg)	0
	(5-1)	

1893
6	at Virginia	0
6	at Penn	18
32	Pitt	0
36	at Bucknell	18
12	at Pittsburgh A. C.	0
	(4-1)	

1894
60	Gettysburg	0
72	Lafayette	0
6	at Navy	6
12	Bucknell (Williamsport)	6
6	at Washington and Jefferson	0
9	at Oberlin	6
14	at Pittsburgh A. C.	0
	(6-0-1)	

1895
48	Gettysburg	0
0	at Cornell	0
16	Bucknell (Williamsport)	0
4	at Penn	35
10	at Pittsburgh A. C.	11
6	at Washington and Jefferson	6
8	at Western Reserve	8
	(2-2-3)	

NOTE: Penn State football teams were without a formal head coach for the first five years of their existence. Cities and towns in parenthesis indicate neutral sites.

1896
Dr. S. B. Newton, Coach

40	Gettysburg	0
10	Pitt	4
8	Dickinson	0
0	at Princeton	39
0	Bucknell (Williamsport)	10
0	at Penn	27
5	Carlisle Indians (Harrisburg)	48

(3-4)

1897

32	Gettysburg	0
0	at Lafayette	24
0	at Princeton	34
0	at Penn	24
0	at Navy	4
0	at Cornell	45
27	Bucknell (Williamsport)	4
10	Bloomsburg Normal	0
0	Dickinson (Sunbury)	6

(3-6)

1898

47	Gettysburg	0
0	at Penn	40
5	at Lafayette	0
45	Susquehanna	6
11	at Navy	16
0	at Princeton	5
5	Duquesne A. C. (Pittsburgh)	18
16	Bucknell (Williamsport)	0
11	at Washington and Jefferson	6
34	Dickinson (Williamsport)	0

(6-4)

1899
Sam Boyle, Coach

38	Mansfield	0
40	Gettysburg	0
6	at Army	0
0	at Princeton	12
0	at Navy	6
15	Dickinson	0
0	Bucknell (Williamsport)	5
0	at Yale	42
0	at Penn	47
5	Duquesne A. C. (Pittsburgh)	64

(4-6)

1900
W. N. Golden, Coach

17	Susquehanna	0
12	Pitt (Bellefonte)	0
0	at Army	0
0	at Princeton	26
5	at Penn	17
0	at Dickinson	18
0	Duquesne A. C. (Pittsburgh)	29
6	Bucknell (Williamsport)	0
0	at Navy	44
44	Gettysburg	0
0	at Buffalo	10

(4-6-1)

1901

17	Susquehanna	0
27	Pitt (Bellefonte)	0
6	at Penn	23
0	at Yale	22
11	at Navy	6
0	Homestead A. C. (Pittsburgh)	39
39	Lehigh (Williamsport)	0
12	Dickinson	0

(5-3)

1902

28	Dickinson Seminary	0
27	Pitt	0
0	at Penn	17
32	Villanova	0
0	at Yale	11
55	Susquehanna	0
6	at Navy	0
39	Gettysburg	0
23	at Dickinson	0
5	at Steelton YMCA	6

(7-3)

1903
Dan Reed, Coach

60	Dickinson Seminary	0
24	Allegheny	5
0	at Penn	39
0	at Yale	27
59	at Pitt	0
17	at Navy	0
0	Dickinson (Williamsport)	6
22	Washington and Jefferson (Pitt.)	0

(5-3)

1904
Tom Fennell, Coach

0	at Penn	6
50	Allegheny	0
0	at Yale	24
34	West Virginia	0
12	Washington and Jefferson (Pitt.)	0
30	Jersey Shore	0
9	at Navy	20
11	Dickinson (Williamsport)	0
44	Geneva	0
5	at Pitt	22

(6-4)

1905

23	Lebanon Valley	0
29	California State	0
0	Carlisle Indians (Harrisburg)	11
18	Gettysburg	0
0	at Yale	12
29	Villanova	0
5	at Navy	11
73	Geneva	0
6	Dickinson (Williamsport)	0
6	West Virginia	0
6	at Pitt	0

(8-3)

1906

24	Lebanon Valley	0
26	Allegheny	0
4	Carlisle Indians (Williamsport)	0
0	Gettysburg	0
12	Bellefonte Academy	0
0	at Yale	10
5	at Navy	0
6	Dickinson (Williamsport)	0
10	West Virginia	0
6	at Pitt	0

(8-1-1)

1907

27	Altoona AA	0
34	Geneva	0
5	Carlisle Indians (Williamsport)	18
46	Grove City	0
8	at Cornell	6
75	Lebanon Valley	0
52	Dickinson (Williamsport)	0
0	at Penn	28
4	at Navy	6
0	at Pitt	6

(6-4)

1908

5	Bellefonte Academy	6
31	Grove City	0
5	Carlisle Indians (Wilkes-Barre)	12
0	at Penn	6
51	Geneva	0
12	West Virginia	0
4	at Cornell	10
33	Bucknell	6
0	at Navy	5
12	at Pitt	6

(5-5)

1909
Bill Hollenback, Coach

31	Grove City	0
8	Carlisle Indians (Wilkes-Barre)	8
46	Geneva	0
3	at Penn	3
33	at Bucknell	0
40	West Virginia	0
5	at Pitt	0

(5-0-2)

1910
Jack Hollenback, Coach

58	Harrisburg AC	0
61	Carnegie Tech	0
45	Sterling AC	0
0	at Penn	10
0	Villanova	0
34	St. Bonaventure	0
45	Bucknell	3
0	at Pitt	11

(5-2-1)

1911
Bill Hollenback, Coach

57	Geneva	0
31	Gettysburg	0
5	at Cornell	0
18	Villanova	0
22	at Penn	6
46	St. Bonaventure	0
17	Colgate	9
0	at Navy	0
3	at Pitt	0

(8-0-1)

1912

41	Carnegie Tech	0
30	Washington and Jefferson	0
29	at Cornell	6
25	Gettysburg	0
14	at Penn	0
71	Villanova	0
37	at Ohio State	0
38	at Pitt	0

(8-0)

1913

49	Carnegie Tech	0
16	Gettysburg	0
0	at Washington and Jefferson	17
0	at Harvard	29
0	at Penn	17
7	Notre Dame	14
0	at Navy	10
6	at Pitt	7

(2-6)

1914

13	Westminster	0
22	Muhlenberg	0
13	Gettysburg	0
30	Ursinus	0
13	at Harvard	13
17	at Lafayette	0
7	at Lehigh	20
3	Michigan State	6
3	at Pitt	13

(5-3-1)

1915
Dick Harlow, Coach

26	Westminster	0
13	Lebanon Valley	0
13	at Penn	3
27	Gettysburg	12
28	West Virginia Wesleyan	0
0	at Harvard	13
7	Lehigh	0
33	at Lafayette	3
0	at Pitt	20

(7-2)

1916

27	Susquehanna	0
55	Westminster	0
50	Bucknell	7
39	West Virginia Wesleyan	0
0	at Penn	15
48	Gettysburg	2
79	Geneva	0
10	at Lehigh	7
40	Lafayette	0
0	at Pitt	31

(8-2)

1917

10	Army Ambulance Corps (Allentown)	0
80	Gettysburg	0
99	St. Bonaventure	0
0	at Washington and Jefferson	7
8	West Virginia Wesleyan	7
7	at Dartmouth	10
0	Lehigh	9
57	Maryland	0
6	at Pitt	28

(5-4)

1918
Hugo Bezdek, Coach

6	Wissahickon Barracks	6
3	Rutgers	26
7	at Lehigh	6
6	at Pitt	28

(1-2-1)

1919

33	Gettysburg	0
9	Bucknell	0
13	at Dartmouth	19
48	Ursinus	7
10	at Penn	0
20	Lehigh	7
20	at Cornell	0
20	at Pitt	0

(7-1)

1920

27	Muhlenberg	7
13	Gettysburg	0
14	Dartmouth	7
41	North Carolina State	0
109	Lebanon Valley	7
28	at Penn	7
20	Nebraska	0
7	at Lehigh	7
0	at Pitt	0

(7-0-2)

1921

53	Lebanon Valley	0
24	Gettysburg	0
35	North Carolina State	0
28	Lehigh	7
21	at Harvard	21
28	Georgia Tech (New York)	7
28	Carnegie Tech	7
13	Navy (Philadelphia)	7
0	at Pitt	0
21	at Washington	7

(8-0-2)

1922

54	St. Bonaventure	0
27	William and Mary	7
20	Gettysburg	0
32	Lebanon Valley	6
33	Middlebury	0
0	Syracuse (New York City)	0
0	Navy (Washington)	14
10	Carnegie Tech	0
6	at Penn	7
0	at Pitt	14
	ROSE BOWL	
3	Southern Cal	14

1923

58	Lebanon Valley	0
16	North Carolina State	0
20	Gettysburg	0
21	Navy	3
13	West Virginia (New York)	13
0	at Syracuse	10
7	Georgia Tech	0
21	at Penn	0
3	at Pitt	20

(6-2-1)

1924

47	Lebanon Valley	3
51	North Carolina State	6
26	Gettysburg	0
13	at Georgia Tech	15
6	Syracuse	10
6	at Navy	0
22	Carnegie Tech	7
0	at Penn	0
28	Marietta	0
3	at Pitt	24

(6-3-1)

1925

14	Lebanon Valley	0
13	Franklin and Marshall	0
7	Georgia Tech (New York)	16
13	Marietta	0
13	Michigan State	6
0	at Syracuse	7
0	Notre Dame	0
0	at West Virginia	14
7	at Pitt	23

(4-4-1)

1926

82	Susquehanna	0
35	Lebanon Valley	0
48	Marietta	6
0	at Notre Dame	28
0	Syracuse	10
20	George Washington	12
0	at Penn	3
9	Bucknell	0
6	at Pitt	24

(5-4)

1927

27	Lebanon Valley	0
34	Gettysburg	13
7	Bucknell	13
20	at Penn	0
9	at Syracuse	6
40	Lafayette	6
13	NYU	13
0	at Pitt	30

(6-2-1)

1928

25	Lebanon Valley	0
12	Gettysburg	0
0	Bucknell	6
0	at Penn	14
6	Syracuse	6
0	Notre Dame (Philadelphia)	9
50	George Washington	0
0	at Lafayette	7
0	at Pitt	26

(3-5-1)

1929

16	Niagara	0
15	Lebanon Valley	0
26	Marshall	7
0	at NYU	7
6	Lafayette	3
6	at Syracuse	4
19	at Penn	7
6	Bucknell	27
7	at Pitt	20

(6-3)

1930
Bob Higgins, Coach

31	Niagara	14
27	Lebanon Valley	0
65	Marshall	0
0	at Lafayette	0
0	Colgate	40
7	at Bucknell	19
0	Syracuse	0
0	at Iowa	19
12	at Pitt	19

(3-4-2)

1931

0	Waynesburg	7
19	Lebanon Valley	6
0	at Temple	12
6	Dickinson	10
0	at Syracuse	7
6	Pitt	41
7	Colgate	32
0	at Lafayette	33
0	at West Virginia	9
31	Lehigh (Philadelphia)	0

(2-8)

1932

27	Lebanon Valley	0
6	Waynesburg	7
13	at Harvard	46
6	Syracuse	12
0	at Colgate	31
18	Sewanee	6
12	at Temple	13

(2-5)

1933

32	Lebanon Valley	6
0	Muhlenberg	3
33	Lehigh	0
0	at Columbia	33
6	at Syracuse	12
40	Johns Hopkins	6
6	at Penn	6

(3-3-1)

1934

13	Lebanon Valley	0
32	Gettysburg	6
31	at Lehigh	0
7	at Columbia	14
0	Syracuse	16
0	at Penn	3
25	Lafayette	6
7	Bucknell	13

(4-4)

1935

12	Lebanon Valley	6
2	Western Maryland	0
26	Lehigh	0
0	at Pitt	9
3	at Syracuse	7
27	Villanova	13
6	at Penn	33
0	at Bucknell	2

(4-4)

1936

45	Muhlenberg	0
0	Villanova	13
6	at Lehigh	7
7	at Cornell	13
18	Syracuse	0
7	at Pitt	34
12	at Penn	19
14	Bucknell	0

(3-5)

	1937	
19	at Cornell	26
32	Gettysburg	6
30	Bucknell	14
14	Lehigh	7
13	at Syracuse	19
7	at Penn	0
21	Maryland	14
7	at Pitt	28
	(5-3)	

	1938	
33	Maryland	0
0	Bucknell	14
59	at Lehigh	6
6	at Cornell	21
33	Syracuse	6
0	Lafayette	7
7	at Penn	7
0	at Pitt	26
	(3-4-1)	

	1939	
13	Bucknell	3
49	Lehigh	7
0	at Cornell	47
6	at Syracuse	6
12	Maryland	0
10	at Penn	0
14	at Army	14
10	Pitt	0
	(5-1-2)	

	1940	
9	Bucknell	0
17	West Virginia	13
34	at Lehigh	0
18	at Temple	0
12	South Carolina	0
13	at Syracuse	13
25	NYU	0
7	at Pitt	20
	(6-1-1)	

	1941	
0	Colgate (Buffalo)	7
27	Bucknell	13
0	at Temple	14
40	Lehigh	6
42	at NYU	0
34	Syracuse	19
7	West Virginia	0

31	at Pitt	7
19	at South Carolina	12
	(7-2)	

	1942	
14	Bucknell	7
19	at Lehigh	3
0	at Cornell	0
13	Colgate	10
0	at West Virginia	24
18	Syracuse	13
13	at Penn	7
14	Pitt	6
	(6-1-1)	

	1943	
14	Bucknell	0
0	at North Carolina	19
0	Colgate	0
6	at Navy	14
45	at Maryland	0
32	West Virginia	7
0	at Cornell	13
13	Temple	0
14	at Pitt	0
	(5-3-1)	

	1944	
58	Muhlenberg	13
14	at Navy	55
20	Bucknell	6
6	at Colgate	0
27	West Virginia	28
41	at Syracuse	0
7	at Temple	6
34	Maryland	19
0	at Pitt	14
	(6-3)	

	1945	
47	Muhlenberg	7
27	Colgate	7
0	at Navy	28
46	at Bucknell	7
26	Syracuse	0
27	Temple	0
0	at Michigan State	33
0	at Pitt	7
	(5-3)	

1946

48	Bucknell	6
9	at Syracuse	0
16	Michigan State	19
6	at Colgate	2
68	Fordham	0
26	Temple	0
12	at Navy	7
7	at Pitt	14

(6-2)

1947

27	Washington State (Hershey)	6
54	Bucknell	0
75	at Fordham	0
40	Syracuse	0
21	West Virginia	14
46	Colgate	0
7	at Temple	0
20	Navy (Baltimore)	7
29	at Pitt	0

COTTON BOWL

13	Southern Methodist	13

(9-0-1)

1948

35	Bucknell	0
34	at Syracuse	14
37	West Virginia	7
14	Michigan State	14
32	at Colgate	13
13	at Penn	0
47	Temple	0
0	at Pitt	7
7	at Washington State	0

(7-1-1)

1949

Joe Bedenk, Coach

6	Villanova	27
7	at Army	42
32	Boston College	14
22	Nebraska	7
0	at Michigan State	24
33	Syracuse	21
34	at West Virginia	14
28	at Temple	7
0	at Pitt	19

(5-4)

1950

Rip Engle, Coach

34	Georgetown	14
7	at Army	41
7	at Syracuse	27
0	at Nebraska	19
7	Temple	7
20	at Boston College	13
27	West Virginia	0
18	Rutgers	14
21	at Pitt	20

(5-3-1)

1951

40	Boston University	34
14	Villanova (Allentown)	20
15	at Nebraska	7
21	Michigan State	32
13	West Virginia	7
0	at Purdue	28
32	Syracuse	13
13	at Rutgers	7
7	at Pitt	13

(5-4)

1952

20	Temple	13
20	Purdue	20
35	William and Mary	23
35	at West Virginia	21
10	Nebraska	0
7	at Michigan State	34
14	at Penn	7
7	at Syracuse	25
7	Rutgers	6
17	at Pitt	0

(7-2-1)

1953

0	at Wisconsin	20
7	at Penn	13
35	at Boston University	13
20	Syracuse	14
27	Texas Christian	21
19	West Virginia	20
28	Fordham	21
54	at Rutgers	26
17	at Pitt	0

(6-3)

1954

14	at Illinois	12
13	at Syracuse	0
34	Virginia	7
14	West Virginia	19
7	at Texas Christian	20
35	at Penn	13
39	Holy Cross	7
37	Rutgers	14
13	at Pitt	0

(7-2)

1955

35	Boston University	0
6	at Army	35
26	Virginia (Richmond)	7
14	Navy	34
7	at West Virginia	21
20	at Penn	0
21	Syracuse	20
34	at Rutgers	13
0	Pitt	20

(5-4)

1956

34	at Penn	0
7	at Army	14
43	Holy Cross	0
7	at Ohio State	6
16	West Virginia	6
9	at Syracuse	13
40	Boston University	7
14	North Carolina State	7
7	at Pitt	7

(6-2-1)

1957

19	at Penn	14
13	Army	27
21	William and Mary	13
20	Vanderbilt	32
20	at Syracuse	12
27	West Virginia	6
20	at Marquette	7
14	at Holy Cross	10
13	at Pitt	14

(6-3)

1958

7	at Nebraska	14
43	at Penn	0
0	at Army	26
40	Marquette	8
34	at Boston University	0
6	Syracuse	14
36	Furman	0
14	at West Virginia	14
32	Holy Cross	0
25	at Pitt	21

(6-3-1)

1959

19	at Missouri	8
21	VMI	0
58	Colgate	20
17	at Army	11
21	Boston University	12
20	Illinois (Cleveland)	9
28	at West Virginia	10
18	Syracuse	20
46	Holy Cross	0
7	at Pitt	22

LIBERTY BOWL

7	Alabama	0

(9-2)

1960

20	Boston University	0
8	Missouri	21
27	at Army	16
15	at Syracuse	21
8	at Illinois	10
34	West Virginia	13
28	Maryland	9
33	at Holy Cross	8
14	at Pitt	3

LIBERTY BOWL

41	Oregon	12

(7-3)

1961

20	Navy	10
8	at Miami (Fla.)	25
32	at Boston University	0
6	Army	10
14	Syracuse	0
33	California	16
17	at Maryland	21
20	at West Virginia	6
34	Holy Cross	14
47	at Pitt	26

GATOR BOWL

30	Georgia Tech	15

(8-3)

1962

41	Navy	7
20	Air Force	6
18	at Rice	7
6	at Army	9
20	Syracuse	19
23	at California	21
23	Maryland	7
34	West Virginia	6
48	at Holy Cross	20
16	at Pitt	0

GATOR BOWL

7	Florida	17

(9-2)

1963

17	at Oregon	7
17	UCLA	14
28	Rice	7
7	Army	10
0	at Syracuse	9
20	West Virginia	9
17	at Maryland	15
10	at Ohio State	7
28	Holy Cross	14
21	at Pitt	22

(7-3)

1964

8	Navy	21
14	at UCLA	21
14	Oregon	22
6	at Army	2
14	Syracuse	21
37	at West Virginia	8
17	Maryland	9
27	at Ohio State	0
24	at Houston	7
28	Pitt	0

(6-4)

1965

0	Michigan State	23
22	UCLA	24
17	at Boston College	0
21	at Syracuse	28
44	West Virginia	6
17	at California	21
21	Kent State	6

14	Navy	6
27	at Pitt	30
19	at Maryland	7

(5-5)

1966
Joe Paterno, Coach

15	Maryland	7
8	at Michigan State	42
0	at Army	11
30	Boston College	21
11	at UCLA	49
38	at West Virginia	6
33	California	15
10	Syracuse	12
0	at Georgia Tech	21
48	at Pitt	24

(5-5)

1967

22	at Navy	23
17	at Miami (Fla.)	8
15	UCLA	17
50	at Boston College	28
21	West Virginia	14
29	at Syracuse	20
38	at Maryland	3
13	North Carolina State	8
35	Ohio University	14
42	Pitt	6

GATOR BOWL

17	Florida State	17

(8-2-1)

1968

31	Navy	6
25	Kansas State	9
31	at West Virginia	20
21	at UCLA	6
29	at Boston College	0
28	Army	24
22	Miami (Fla.)	7
57	at Maryland	13
65	at Pitt	9
30	Syracuse	12

ORANGE BOWL

15	Kansas	14

(11-0)

1969

45	at Navy	22
27	Colorado	3
17	at Kansas State	14
20	West Virginia	0
15	at Syracuse	14
42	Ohio University	3
38	Boston College	16
48	Maryland	0
27	at Pitt	7

ORANGE BOWL

10	Missouri	3

(11-0)

1970

55	Navy	7
13	at Colorado	41
16	at Wisconsin	29
28	at Boston College	3
7	Syracuse	24
38	at Army	14
42	West Virginia	8
34	at Maryland	0
32	Ohio University	22
35	Pitt	15

(7-3)

1971

56	at Navy	3
44	at Iowa	14
16	Air Force	14
42	at Army	0
31	at Syracuse	0
66	Texas Christian	14
35	at West Virginia	7
63	Maryland	27
35	North Carolina State	3
55	at Pitt	18
11	at Tennessee	31

COTTON BOWL

30	Texas	6

1972

21	at Tennessee	28
21	Navy	10
14	Iowa	10
35	at Illinois	17
45	at Army	0
17	Syracuse	0
28	at West Virginia	19
46	Maryland	16

45	at Boston College	26
49	Pitt	27

SUGAR BOWL

0	Oklahoma	14

(10-2)

1973

20	at Stanford	6
39	at Navy	0
27	Iowa	8
19	at Air Force	9
54	Army	3
49	at Syracuse	6
62	West Virginia	14
42	Maryland	22
35	North Carolina State	29
49	Ohio University	10
35	Pitt	13

ORANGE BOWL

16	LSU	9

(12-0)

1974

24	Stanford	20
6	Navy	7
27	at Iowa	0
21	at Army	14
55	Wake Forest	0
30	Syracuse	14
21	at West Virginia	12
24	Maryland	17
7	at North Carolina State	12
35	Ohio University	16
31	at Pitt	10

COTTON BOWL

41	Baylor	20

(10-2)

1975

26	Temple (Philadelphia)	25
34	Stanford	14
9	at Ohio State	17
30	at Iowa	10
10	Kentucky	3
39	West Virginia	0
19	at Syracuse	7
31	Army	0
15	at Maryland	13
14	North Carolina State	15
7	at Pitt	6

SUGAR BOWL

6	Alabama	13

(9-3)

A History of Greatness (Penn State Records)

1976

15	Stanford	12
7	Ohio State	12
6	Iowa	7
6	at Kentucky	22
38	Army	16
27	Syracuse	3
33	at West Virginia	0
31	at Temple	30
41	North Carolina State	20
21	at Miami (Fla.)	7
6	at Pitt	24
	GATOR BOWL	
9	Notre Dame	20
	(7-5)	

1977

45	at Rutgers	7
31	Houston	14
27	Maryland	9
20	Kentucky	24
16	Utah State	7
31	at Syracuse	24
49	West Virginia	28
49	Miami (Fla.)	7
21	at North Carolina State	17
44	Temple	7
15	at Pitt	13
	FIESTA BOWL	
42	Arizona State	30
	(11-1)	

1978

10	at Temple	7
26	Rutgers	10
19	at Ohio State	0
26	Southern Methodist	21
58	Texas Christian	0
30	at Kentucky	0
45	Syracuse	15
49	at West Virginia	21
27	Maryland	3
19	North Carolina State	10
17	Pittsburgh	10
	SUGAR BOWL	
7	Alabama	14
	(11-1)	

1979

45	Rutgers	10
14	Texas A&M	27
17	at Nebraska	42
27	at Maryland	7
24	Army	3
35	Syracuse	7
31	West Virginia	6
10	Miami (Fla.)	26
9	at North Carolina State	7
22	Temple	7
14	Pitt	29
	LIBERTY BOWL	
9	Tulane	7
	(8-4)	

1980

54	Colgate	10
25	at Texas A&M	9
7	Nebraska	21
29	at Missouri	21
24	at Maryland	10
24	at Syracuse	7
20	at West Virginia	15
27	Miami (Fla.)	12
21	North Carolina State	13
50	at Temple	7
9	Pitt	14
	FIESTA BOWL	
31	Ohio State	7
	(10-2)	

1981

52	Cincinnati	0
30	at Nebraska	24
30	Temple	0
38	Boston College	7
41	at Syracuse	16
30	West Virginia	7
14	at Miami (Fla.)	17
22	at North Carolina State	15
16	Alabama	31
24	Notre Dame	21
48	at Pitt	14
	FIESTA BOWL	
26	Southern Cal	10

ALL-TIME PENN STATE INDIVIDUAL RECORDS
(through 1981 season)

RUSHING

Career

	Att.	Yards	Avg.	TDs
Lydell Mitchell (1969-71)	501	2934	5.9	38
Matt Suhey (1976-79)	633	2818	4.5	26
John Cappelletti (1972-73)	519	2639	5.1	29
Lenny Moore (1953-55)	382	2380	6.2	24
Curt Warner (1979-81)	451	2357	5.2	16
Charlie Pittman (1967-69)	454	2236	4.9	30
Booker Moore (1977-80)	448	2072	4.6	20
Franco Harris (1969-71)	380	2002	5.3	24
Fran Rogel (1947-49)	—	1501	—	—
Roger Kochman (1959, 1961-62)	242	1480	5.6	12

Season

	Att.	Yards	Avg.	TDs
Lydell Mitchell, 1971	254	1567	6.2	26
John Cappelletti, 1973	286	1522	5.3	17
John Cappelletti, 1972	233	1117	4.8	12
Lenny Moore, 1954	136	1082	8.0	12
Curt Warner, 1981	171	1044	6.1	8
Matt Suhey, 1979	185	973	5.3	6
Charlie Pittman, 1968	186	950	5.1	14
Curt Warner, 1980	196	922	4.7	6
Dave McNaughton, 1965	193	884	4.6	7
Tom Donchez, 1974	195	880	4.5	7

PASSING

Career

	Att.	Comp.	Pct.	Yards	TDs	Int.
Chuck Fusina (1975-78)	665	371	55.8	5382	37	32
John Hufnagel (1970-72)	408	225	55.1	3545	26	17
Tom Shuman (1972-74)	365	188	51.5	2886	22	18
Todd Blackledge (1980-81)	366	180	49.2	2594	19	27
Tom Sherman (1965-67)	347	163	47.0	2588	19	14
Tony Rados (1951-53)	425	199	46.8	2437	—	—
Pete Liske (1961-63)	355	195	54.9	2370	24	10
Chuck Burkhart (1967-69)	312	152	48.7	2076	7	16
Rich Lucas (1957-59)	256	121	47.2	1822	12	16
Galen Hall (1959-61)	222	107	47.2	1619	15	11

Lydell Mitchell is the career rushing leader for Penn State with almost 3,000 yards.

PASSING (con't)

Season

	Att.	Comp.	Pct.	Yards	TDs	Int.
Chuck Fusina, 1977	246	142	57.7	2221	15	9
John Hufnagel, 1972	216	115	53.2	2039	15	8
Chuck Fusina, 1978	242	137	56.6	1859	11	12
Tom Sherman, 1967	205	104	50.7	1616	13	9
Todd Blackledge, 1981	207	104	50.2	1557	12	14
Tom Shuman, 1973	161	83	51.6	1375	13	5
Tom Shuman, 1974	183	97	53.0	1355	6	12
Jack White, 1965	205	98	47.8	1275	6	14
Chuck Fusina, 1976	167	88	52.7	1260	11	10
John Hufnagel, 1971	136	86	63.2	1185	10	6

RECEIVING

Career

	Receptions	Yards	%Avg.	TDs
Jack Curry (1965-67)	117	1837	15.7	5
Ted Kwalick (1966-68)	86	1343	15.6	10
Dan Natale (1971-73)	67	1038	15.5	8
Mickey Shuler (1975-77)	66	1016	15.4	4
Junior Powell (1961-63)	65	866	13.3	8
Scott Fitzkee (1975-78)	65	1263	19.4	11
Brad Scovill (1978-80)	58	813	14.0	6
Tom Donovan (1975-76, 78-79)	57	1058	15.2	4
Jimmy Cefalo (1974-77)	56	1085	18.9	7
Greg Edmonds (1968-70)	56	860	15.4	6

Season

	Receptions	Yards	Avg.	TDs
Jack Curry, 1965	42	572	13.6	2
Jack Curry, 1967	41	681	16.6	2
Greg Edmonds, 1970	38	506	13.3	6
Scott Fitzkee, 1978	37	630	17.0	6
Jack Curry, 1966	34	584	17.2	1
Ted Kwalick, 1967	33	563	17.1	4
Mickey Shuler, 1977	33	600	18.2	1
Junior Powell, 1962	32	303	9.5	3
Ted Kwalick, 1968	31	403	13.0	2
Gary Hayman, 1973	30	525	17.5	3
Dan Natale, 1972	30	460	14.4	5
Bob Parsons, 1970	30	489	16.3	5
Jim Garrity, 1954	30	349	11.6	3

LEADERS BY SEASON

Rushing

Season	Player	Att.	Yards	Avg.	TDs
1981	Curt Warner	171	1044	6.1	8
1980	Curt Warner	196	922	4.7	6
1979	Matt Suhey	185	973	5.3	6
1978	Matt Suhey	184	720	3.9	7
1977	Matt Suhey	139	638	4.6	8
1976	Steve Geise	116	560	4.8	3
1975	Woody Petchel	148	621	4.2	5
1974	Tom Donchez	195	880	4.5	7
1973	John Cappelletti	286	1522	5.3	17
1972	John Cappelletti	233	1117	4.8	12
1971	Lydell Mitchell	254	1567	6.2	26
1970	Lydell Mitchell	134	751	5.6	6
1969	Charlie Pittman	149	706	4.7	10
1968	Charlie Pittman	186	950	5.1	14
1967	Charlie Pittman	119	580	4.9	6
1966	Bob Campbell	79	498	6.1	5
1965	Dave McNaughton	193	884	4.6	7
1964	Tom Urbanik	134	625	4.7	8
1963	Gary Klingensmith	102	450	4.4	3
1962	Roger Kochman	120	652	5.4	4
1961	Roger Kochman	129	666	5.2	6
1960	Jim Kerr	93	389	4.2	6
1959	Rich Lucas	99	325	3.3	6
1958	Dave Kasperian	98	381	3.9	5
1957	Dave Kasperian	122	469	3.8	7
1956	Billy Kane	105	530	5.0	7

Passing

Season	Player	Att.	Comp.	Yards	TDs	Int.
1981	Todd Blackledge	207	104	1557	12	14
1980	Todd Blackledge	159	76	1037	7	13
1979	Dayle Tate	176	92	1179	8	11
1978	Chuck Fusina	242	137	1859	11	12
1977	Chuck Fusina	246	142	2221	15	9
1976	Chuck Fusina	167	88	1260	11	10
1975	John Andress	149	71	991	2	4
1974	Tom Shuman	183	97	1355	6	12
1973	Tom Shuman	161	83	1375	13	5
1972	John Hufnagel	216	115	2039	15	8
1971	John Hufnagel	136	86	1185	10	6
1970	Mike Cooper	64	32	429	4	6

Passing (con't)

Season	Player	Att.	Yards	Avg.	TDs	Int.
1969	Chuck Burkhart	114	59	805	1	9
1968	Chuck Burkhart	177	87	1170	6	7
1967	Tom Sherman	205	104	1616	13	9
1966	Tom Sherman	135	58	943	6	4
1965	Jack White	205	98	1275	6	14
1964	Gary Wydman	149	70	832	1	6
1963	Pete Liske	161	87	1117	10	5
1962	Pete Liske	162	91	1037	12	4
1961	Galen Hall	97	50	951	8	5
1960	Galen Hall	89	39	448	5	5
1959	Rich Lucas	117	58	913	2	8
1958	Rich Lucas	80	36	483	3	4
1957	Al Jacks	103	53	673	5	3
1956	Milt Plum	75	40	675	6	7

Receiving

Season	Player	Receptions	Yards	Avg.	TDs
1981	Gregg Garrity	23	415	18.0	1
1980	Kenny Jackson	21	386	18.4	5
1979	Brad Scovill	26	331	12.7	3
1978	Scott Fitzkee	37	630	17.0	6
1977	Mickey Shuler	33	600	18.2	1
1976	Mickey Shuler	21	281	12.9	3
1975	Dick Barvinchak	17	327	14.2	0
1974	Jerry Jeram	17	259	15.2	2
	Tom Donchez	17	176	10.4	1
1973	Gary Hayman	30	525	17.5	3
1972	Dan Natale	30	460	15.3	5
1971	Bob Parsons	30	489	15.6	5
1970	Greg Edmonds	38	506	13.3	6
1969	Greg Edmonds	20	246	12.3	0
1968	Ted Kwalick	31	403	13.0	2
1967	Jack Curry	41	681	16.9	2
1966	Jack Curry	34	584	17.2	1
1965	Jack Curry	42	572	13.6	2
1964	Bill Huber	25	347	13.9	1
1963	Dick Anderson	21	229	10.9	2
1962	Junior Powell	32	303	9.5	3
1961	Jim Schwab	16	257	16.1	0
1960	Jim Kerr	13	163	12.5	2
	Henry Opperman	13	131	10.1	1
1959	Dick Hoak	14	167	11.9	0
1958	Maurice Schleicher	9	127	14.1	0
	Dave Kasperian	9	107	11.9	2
	Norm Neff	9	106	11.8	2
1957	Les Walters	24	440	18.3	5
1956	Billy Kane	16	132	8.3	0

A History of Greatness (Penn State Records)

Scoring

Season	Player	Points	TDs	PAT-K	FG
1981	Brian Franco	81	0	36-37	15
1980	Herb Menhardt	71	0	26-26	15
1979	Herb Menhardt	70	0	28-28	14
1978	Matt Bahr	97	0	31-31	22
1977	Matt Bahr	81	0	39-41	14
1976	Mike Guman	48	8	0-0	0
1975	Chris Bahr	73	0	19-20	18
1974	Tom Donchez	48	8	0-0	0
1973	John Cappelletti	102	17	0-0	0
1972	John Cappelletti	78	13	0-0	0
1971	Lydell Mitchell	174	29	0-0	0
1970	Franco Harris	48	8	0-0	0
1969	Charlie Pittman	66	11	0-0	0
1968	Charlie Pittman	84	14	0-0	0
1967	Don Abbey	88	9	23-26 (a)	3
1966	Tom Sherman	57	5	7-10 (a)	6
1965	Mike Irwin	42	7	0-0	0
	Dave McNaughton	42	7	0-0	0
1964	Tom Urbanik	48	8	0-0	0
1963	Ron Coates	33	0	18-19	5
1962	Roger Kochman	48	8	0-0	0
1961	Roger Kochman	56	9	0-0 (a)	0
1960	Jim Kerr	52	8	0-0 (b)	—

(a) — does not include one two-point conversion
(b) — does not include two two-point conversions

All-Pro Pittsburgh Steeler great, Franco Harris, gained over 2,000 career yards for Penn State during the 1969-1971 seasons.

ALL-AMERICA SELECTIONS
(through 1981)

Penn State has had 46 football players named to someone's All-America first team, 39 since the end of World War II. The most notable absence is Lenny Moore, one of the great running backs in college football history and a member of the pro football Hall of Fame. The strangest presence is John Nessel, an offensive lineman who was selected after a 1974 season in which he was not a regular player.

Moore's absence can be explained by lack of publicity; Nessel's presence by the enormous amount of attention the Nittany Lions were getting by the mid-1970s and the fact that only a handful of people in the country should be allowed to vote for offensive linemen.

The chosen multitude:

W.T. (Mother) Dunn, center, 1906 — Selected by Walter Camp after senior season in which team went 8-1-1. Practiced medicine in Hawaii for many years before his death in 1962.

Bob Higgins, end, 1919 — A Walter Camp choice who later served as head coach for 19 years at his alma mater. One of only five players in the school's history to earn five letters in football. Also lettered in baseball, boxing and wrestling. Played pro ball for Canton Bulldogs for two seasons. Father-in-law of All-America guard Steve Suhey, grandfather of State players Matt, Paul and Larry Suhey. Inducted in National Football foundation Hall of Fame in 1954, Higgins died in 1969.

Charley Way, halfback, 1920 — This retired employee of the Internal Revenue Service who lives in Thorndale, Pa., was another Walter Camp choice.

Glenn Killinger, halfback, 1921 — Earned nine college letters in football, baseball and basketball. Led Nittany Lions to unbeaten seasons his junior and senior seasons. Later played pro football with the New York Giants and pro baseball with the Yankees before settling into long career as football coach and athletic director at West Chester (Pa.) State. Another college football Hall of Famer.

Joe Bedenk, guard, 1923 — Longtime Nittany Lion baseball coach was picked by Walter Camp. Served as head football coach for one year (1949) between successful stints of Bob Higgins and Rip Engle. Died in State College in 1978.

Harry Wilson, halfback, 1923 — Chosen by 500 Coaches and Percy Haughton after scoring every Nittany Lion touchdown in the final six games of the 1923 season. Finished his career at Army, then served as Air Force pilot commander during World War II, when he flew 45 successful combat missions. Inducted into the National Football Foundation Hall of Fame in 1973, passed away in Florida five years later.

Leon Gajecki, center, 1940 — Outstanding player on 6-1-1 Nittany Lion team and selected by NEA because of it. Later worked for Humble Oil, is now retired and living in Pitman, N.J.

Steve Suhey, guard, 1947 — Chosen by Collier's, Associated Press and International News Service, Suhey was a standout on the 1948 Cotton Bowl team. Later played for the Pittsburgh Steelers for two seasons. Three of his sons played football at Penn State and one, Matt, is a fullback for the Chicago Bears. Sold college jewelry and lived in State College until his death in 1977.

Sam Tamburo, end, 1948 — Another Cotton Bowl star who later played for the Bulldogs and Giants in the NFL. Picked by both Collier's and INS. Works for the Internal Revenue Service and lives in New Kensington, Pa.

Sam Valentine, guard, 1956 — A pick of the Football Writers Association of America for Look magazine, Valentine is now a division manager for Chicago-based BMI, Inc., and lives in Michigan City, Ind.

Richie Lucas, quarterback, 1959 — Riverboat Richie was runnerup to Dr. Billy Cannon for the Heisman Trophy, first Penn Stater to come so close to that award. Among those All-America squads he made were United Press International, United States Coaches Association, Sporting News, NEA and Football News. The first choice in the Buffalo Bills' draft, Lucas played two years as a defensive back in the pros. He is an assistant athletic director at Penn State.

Bob Mitinger, end, 1961 — One of two great two-way ends on the early-1960 Lion squads, Bob was chosen by the United States Coaches Association. Played pro ball for the San Diego Chargers and is now an attorney in State College.

Dave Robinson, end, 1962 — The other outstanding two-way end of his era and one of the most complete athletes in Penn State history. Led his Moorestown (N.J.) High team to state basketball championship. Later starred as an All-Pro linebacker for the Green Bay Packers in the Vince Lombardi era. An All-America choice of Associated Press, NEA and Look and Time magazines. Now a salesman living in Akron, Ohio.

Roger Kochman, halfback, 1962 — Led Nittany Lions in rushing both his junior and senior seasons. Never reached full potential because of a series

Dave Robinson earned All-American honors as a two-way end for Penn State in 1962. Later, he starred as an All-Pro linebacker for the Green Bay Packers in the Vince Lombardi era.

of nagging injuries in college. In first pro season, he was victim of a severe leg injury that curtailed promising career. Selected by U.S. Coaches Association. Now works for phone company in Philadelphia and lives in Haverford, Pa.

Glenn Ressler, middle guard, 1964 — The quiet man from Leck Kill, Pa., joined Rich Lucas as Maxwell Club Trophy winner after a senior year that featured a tremendous performance in stunning shutout at Ohio State. All-America choice of the Coaches Association, NEA, Sporting News and Time magazine among others. Was an underrated offensive guard for the Baltimore Colts for ten seasons. Lives in Camp Hill, Pa., where he keeps a watch on his nine restaurants.

Ted Kwalick, tight end, 1967-68 — Penn State's first two-time All-America. Consensus choice both seasons, including selection by AP and UPI. Called "the greatest tight end I've ever seen" during his college days, Kwalick had a successful pro career with the San Francisco 49ers. Owns a night club in the Bay Area.

Dennis Onkotz, linebacker, 1968-69 — Selected by both AP and UPI after his junior and senior seasons, Dennis was a big play linebacker who specialized in punt returns. Injury cut short a promising career with the New York Jets. Now a retirement analyst in State College.

Mike Reid, defensive tackle, 1969 — Nittany Lions' first unanimous All-American choice. Won Outland Trophy, Maxwell Trophy and finished high for a non-skill-position player in Heisman balloting. First round draft choice of the Cincinnati Bengals where he won All-Pro honors. Quit after five seasons to devote full time to career in music. Now a songwriter in Nashville.

Charlie Pittman, running back, 1969 — A choice of the United States Football Coaches after scoring 24 touchdowns as Penn State won 22 consecutive games in his last two seasons. Played one season each with the St. Louis Cardinals and Baltimore Colts. Now is a promotions man for an Erie newspaper.

Neal Smith, safety, 1969 — From walk-on to All-America according to UPI, NEA and the New York Daily News. His 19 career interceptions are a school record and his 10 in 1969 set a Nittany Lion mark later tied by Pete Harris. Now a civil engineer who lives in his native Selinsgrove, Pa.

Jack Ham, linebacker, 1970 — Unwanted by any major college after his senior year in high school, Ham worked his way onto every All-America squad after his senior year. Was prime mover in changing the pro concept of outside linebacker from power to finesse and speed in his early years with the Pittsburgh Steelers. Has four Super Bowl rings. Lives in Pittsburgh.

Dave Joyner, tackle, 1971 — One of the leaders of the team that smashed Texas, 30-6, in the Cotton Bowl, Joyner was rewarded with slots on the UPI, Football News, Gridiron, Walter Camp, American Football Coaches Association and Football Writers All-America squads. He is a graduate of Penn State's Hershey Medical School and is putting the final touches on his preparation for a career in orthopedic surgery.

Lydell Mitchell, running back, 1971 — His 29-touchdown senior season earned him slots on the AP, Football News and Gridiron All-America squads. The all-time leading rusher in Penn State history later became a terrific running back and pass receiver for the Baltimore Colts. Now owns a bar and some restaurants and lives in Baltimore.

Charlie Zapiec, linebacker, 1971 — A starting offensive guard for two seasons, Charlie missed most of the 1970 season after undergoing an emergency appendectomy in Colorado but bounced back to earn NEA All-America honors as a senior. Played many years for the Montreal Alouettes in Canada.

Bruce Bannon, defensive end, 1972 — A gentle geology major off the field and a ferocious pass rusher on it, Bannon was selected by the American Football Coaches, NEA, UPI, Gridiron, Football News and Walter Camp. Has a Super Bowl ring from rookie season with Miami Dolphins. Now lives in Canfield, Ohio, and is in charge of industrial sales development for Reactive Metals, Inc., which specializes in titanium.

John Hufnagel, quarterback, 1972 — Easily the most efficient passer in Nittany Lion history, rewarded with spots on Associated Press and Walter Camp teams after senior year. One of a long list of quarterbacks from McKees Rocks, Pa., including Chuck Burkhart, Tom Clements, Billy Daniels and Chuck Fusina. Played for Denver Broncos for two years before establishing lengthy career in Canadian League.

John Skorupan, linebacker, 1972 — Another reason why Penn State has become known as Linebacker U. John was selected for Associated Press Football Writers and NEA teams after sparkling career as Jack Ham-type collegian. Spent several years in NFL after being drafted by Buffalo Bills.

John Cappelletti, tailback, 1973 — The Heisman Cometh . First Heisman Trophy winner at Penn State after brilliant senior season. Spent sophomore season on defense while Lydell Mitchell and Franco Harris ran the ball. Spent most of NFL career with Los Angeles Rams. Now with San Diego Chargers.

Randy Crowder, defensive tackle, 1973 — Selected by UPI and Football News. Exceptionally quick off the ball. Once almost picked off a straight handoff in opponents' backfield. Now a nose tackle for the Tampa Bay Buccaneers.

Ed O'Neil, linebacker, 1973 — Superb athlete. Quick enough to play defensive back as a college sophomore. Selected by Walter Camp, Sporting News and Time. Enjoyed continued success with Detroit Lions as an inside linebacker.

Mike Hartenstine, defensive tackle, 1974 — If juicy quotes were necessary to make All-America, Mike would have come up short. Let his play do the talking for him and made the grade with AP, UPI, Football Coaches Association and Football Writers. Still a punishing tackler as a Chicago Bear defensive end.

Kicker Chris Bahr earned consensus All-American honors for Penn State in 1975.

John Nessel, offensive lineman, 1974 — Listed as a tackle on Walter Camp squad. Couldn't make All Penn State as senior, however. In fairness to John, the tackles and guards who started ahead of him were Jeff Bleamer, Brad Benson, Tom Rafferty and George Reihner, all of whom enjoyed some success in NFL. Was started as junior. Now a teacher in Ridgefield, Conn.

Chris Bahr, kicker, 1975 — Threatened to hit roof of Louisiana Superdome with his booming punts in the 1975 Sugar Bowl, but became strictly a placekicker in pro career with Cincinnati and Oakland, where he won a Super Bowl ring. Was biggest offensive weapon in his senior year as Lions scored only 20 touchdowns. Chosen by Time, Sporting News, UPI and Walter Camp.

Greg Buttle, linebacker, 1975 — A Jersey shore lifeguard during his college summers, opponents learned to guard their lives when he was in their area during the season. Selected by AP, Football News, Football Writers, Time, UPI, Walter Camp and Sporting News. Has had major role in rebuilding the image of the New York Jets as an outside linebacker.

Tom Rafferty, guard, 1975 — Chosen by Football News and Football Writers after somewhat overlooked career in Lion Country. The Dallas Cowboys didn't miss him, though. Has been a mainstay on Tom Landry's offensive line, first as a guard, then as a center.

Kurt Allerman, linebacker, 1976 — Chosen by United Press International after an outstanding career at Penn State. Never quite reached same heights as a pro after being drafted by the St. Louis Cardinals.

Keith Dorney, Tackle, 1977-78 — An early first-round pick of the Detroit Lions after his college play earned him All-America from Football Writers as a junior, nearly everybody else as a senior. Hasn't disappointed team that drafted him, either, having started every game for Detroit.

Randy Sidler, middle guard, 1977 — Converted tight end. Another silent type who lack of bombast didn't keep him from being recognized by Associated Press after strong senior year. Now an electrical contractor in Danville, Pa.

Matt Bahr, kicker, 1978 — Still does kickin' right, even if it is two places removed from where he made chicken commercial before 1981 pro season. Did kickin' better than anyone in country in both football and soccer his senior year at State. Won regular job as Steeler rookie before moving on to San Francisco and Cleveland in '81.

Bruce Clark, defensive tackle, 1978-79 — A consensus selection both seasons. Seen by the pros as the next great linebacker while he was still in high school at New Castle, Pa., Clark was seen as a defensive lineman by the time he was a junior. Always mumbled about his position. So did opponents who had to line up across from him. The fourth pick overall in the 1979 NFL draft, Clark opted for a Canadian League contract. Expected back in United States football soon.

Bruce Clark was an All-America selection in both 1978 and in 1979 as a defensive tackle for Penn State. His great skills resulted in his being the fourth pick overall in the 1979 NFL draft.

Chuck Fusina, quarterback, 1978 — The Magic Man. Chuck was an amateur magician who came within a few plays of making the Penn State thirst for number one disappear in the 1979 Sugar Bowl. He was honored by the AP, Football Writers, Football Coaches, NEA, UPI and Walter Camp. A middle-round choice of the Tampa Bay Buccaneers, Fusina won his spot with the pro team, backing up Doug Williams.

Pete Harris, safety, 1978 — The next generation's trivia question: Someone named Harris made All-America at Penn State in the '70s. Name him. Easy, Franco. Naw, you're wrong. It was his brother, Pete. Led nation with 10 interceptions as a junior, which got him nod from United Press International.

Matt Millen, defensive tackle, 1978 — Didn't win national championship as a collegian, but did in first year in pros as Oakland Raider starting middle linebacker in Super Bowl XV. This came after injury plagued senior year at Penn State. As a junior, was good enough to make UPI and Walter Camp take notice of his enormous talents.

Bill Dugan, tackle, 1980 — punishing blocker who was chosen by the Football Coaches Association. He played in 1981 for the Seattle Seahawks.

Sean Farrell, offensive guard, 1980-81 — The most celebrated offensive lineman in Nittany Lion history. Made the Football News All-America team as a junior, then made every team as a senior. First round draft choice of the Tampa Bay Buccaneers in 1982.

Curt Warner, running back, 1981 — Selected by both United Press International and Walter Camp after brilliant junior season. Has excellent chance, barring injuries, to graduate as the all time leading rusher at Penn State.

Matt Millen earned All-American honors as a tackle for Penn State in 1978. In his first year in the pros as the starting middle linebacker for the Oakland Raiders, Millen earned a championship ring in Super Bowl XV.

Barring injuries Curt Warner—who won All-American honors as a junior in 1981—has an excellent chance of graduating as the all-time leading rusher in Penn State History.

PENN STATE AND THE BOWLS

The 26-10 victory over Southern Cal in the 1982 Fiesta Bowl marked the 20th bowl appearance and 12th victory (against six losses and two ties) for the Nittany Lions.

The first came in 1923 when Penn State, which had been chosen for the Rose Bowl BEFORE the 1922 season, bowed to the same Trojans, 13-3.

The 1948, State capped an unbeaten, untied season with an appearance in the Cotton Bowl. Two black players, Dennie Hoggard and Wally Triplett, integrated a Southern bowl game for the first time. The Lions ralled to tie Doak Walker's Southern Methodist team, 13-13.

Joe Paterno's unbeaten squads posted back-to-back victories in the Orange Bowl in 1969 and 70, then finished off a third perfect season with a win in Miami in 1974. In 1979, the Lions went into the Sugar Bowl ranked number one but were deprived of their first national championship by Alabama, 14-7.

Other bowl appearances and results:

1959 Liberty Bowl — Penn State 7, Alabama 0.
1960 Liberty Bowl — Penn State 41, Oregon 12.
1961 Gator Bowl — Penn State 30, Georgia Tech 15.
1962 Gator Bowl — Florida 17, Penn State 7.
1967 Gator Bowl — Penn State 17, Florida State 17.
1969 Orange Bowl — Penn State 15, Kansas 14.
1970 Orange Bowl — Penn State 10, Missouri 3.
1972 Cotton Bowl — Penn State 30, Texas 6.
1972 Sugar Bowl — Oklahoma 14, Penn State 0.
1974 Orange Bowl — Penn State 16, Louisiana State 9.
1975 Cotton Bowl — Penn State 41, Baylor 20.
1975 Sugar Bowl — Alabama 13, Penn State 6.
1976 Gator Bowl — Notre Dame 20, Penn State 9.
1977 Fiesta Bowl — Penn State 42, Arizona State 30.
1980 Fiesta Bowl — Penn State 31, Ohio State 19.

BOWL-BY-BOWL RECORDS

	W	L	T	Pct.
Orange	3	0	0	1.000
Cotton	2	0	1	1.000
Rose	0	1	0	.000
Sugar	0	3	0	.000
Fiesta	3	0	0	1.000
Gator	1	2	1	.333
Liberty	3	0	0	1.000
TOTAL	12	6	2	.667

Gregg Buttle, another in a long line of outstanding Penn State linebackers, played in the Orange (1973), Cotton (1974), and Sugar (1975) Bowl games during his three years as a member of the Penn State varsity.

PENN STATERS
IN THE NFL

Doug Allen, linebacker, Buffalo, 1974-75
Kurt Allerman, linebacker, St. Louis, 1977-79, Green Bay, 1980-81
Matt Bahr, kicker, Pittsburgh, 1979-80, San Francisco and Cleveland, 1981
Chris Bahr, kicker, Cincinnati 1976-79, Oakland, 1980-81
Ralph Baker, linebacker, New York Jets, 1964-74.
Bruce Bannon, linebacker, Miami, 1973-74
Stew Barber, tackle, Buffalo, 1961-69
Clarence Beck, tackle, Pottsville, 1925
Brad Benson, tackle, New York Giants, 1978-81
Robert Berryman, back, Frankford, 1924
Jeff Bleamer, tackle, Philadelphia, 1975-76, New York Jets, 1977, New York Giants, 1978
Dave Bradley, guard, Green Bay, 1969-71, St. Louis, 1972
Greg Buttle, linebacker, New York Jets, 1976-81
Rich Buzin, tackle, New York Giants, 1968-70, Los Angeles, 1971, Chicago, 1972
Bob Campbell, running back, Pittsburgh, 1969
John Cappelletti, running back, Los Angeles, 1974-79, San Diego, 1980-81
Frank Case, defensive end, Kansas City, 1981
Jimmy Cefalo, wide receiver, 1979-81
Chuck Cherundolo, center, Cleveland, 1937-39, Philadelphia, 1940, Pittsburgh, 1941-48
Ron Coder, guard, 1976-79, St. Louis, 1980
Larry Conover, center, Toledo, 1921-23, Kenosha, 1924, Akron, 1925
William Cooper, quarterback, Cleveland, 1936-37, Cincinnati, 1937
Chuck Crist, defensive back, New York Giants, 1972-74, New Orleans, 1975-78, San Francisco, 1979
Ron Crosby, linebacker, New Orleans, 1978, Detroit, 1979, New York Jets, 1980-81
Randy Crowder, defensive tackle, Miami, 1974-76, Tampa Bay, 1978-81

Benn Cubbage, Massilon, 1919.
Eric Cunningham, guard, New York Jets, 1979, St. Louis, 1980
Robert Davis, end, Pittsburgh, 1946-50
Tom DePaso, linebacker, Cincinnati, 1978
Chris Devlin, linebacker, Cincinnati, 1975-77
Tom Donchez, fullback, Chicago, 1975-76
Tom Donovan, wide receiver, New Orleans, 1980
Keith Dorney, tackle, Detroit, 1979-81
Chuck Drazenovich, linebacker, Washington, 1950-59
Bill Dugan, tackle, Seattle, 1981
Jeff Durkota, back, Los Angeles, 1948
John Ebersole, linebacker, New York Jets, 1970-77
Herb Eschbach, center, Providence, 1930-31
John Filak, tackle, Frankford, 1927-29
Scott Fitzkee, wide receiver, Philadelphia, 1979-80, San Diego 1981
Len Frketich, tackle, Pittsburgh, 1945
Chuck Fusina, quarterback, Tampa Bay, 1979-81
Charlie Getty, tackle, Kansas City, 1974-81
Gene Gladys, linebacker, New Orleans, 1981
Dave Graf, linebacker, Cleveland, 1975-79
Donn Greenshields, tackle, Brooklyn, 1932-33
Roosevelt Grier, tackle, New York Giants, 1955-62, Los Angeles, 1963-66
Paul Griffiths, guard, Canton, 1921
Mike Guman, running back, Los Angeles, 1980-81
Al Gursky, linebacker, New York Giants, 1963
Hinkey Haines, quarterback, New York, 1925-28, Staton Island, 1929-31
Galen Hall, quarterback, Washington, 1962, New York Jets, 1963
Jack Ham, linebacker, Pittsburgh, 1971-81
Steve Hamas, back, Orange, 1929
Franco Harris, running back, Pittsburgh, 1972-81
Mike Hartenstine, defensive end, Chicago, 1975-81
Gary Hayman, running back, Buffalo, 1974-75
Bob Higgins, end, Canton, 1920-21
Dick Hoak, running back, Pittsburgh, 1961-70
John Hufnagel, quarterback, Denver, 1974-76
Tom Hull, linebacker, San Francisco, 1974, Green Bay, 1975
John Jaffurs, guard, Washington, 1946
Charlie Janerette, guard, Los Angeles, 1961, New York Giants, 1960-61,
    New York Jets, 1963, Denver, 1964-65
Larry Joe, back, Buffalo, 1949
Don Jonas, back, Philadelphia, 1962
Jim Kerr, defensive back, Washington, 1961-62
Glenn Killinger, back, New York Giants, 1926

John Klotz, tackle, New York Titans, 1962, San Diego, 1962, New York Jets, 1963, Houston, 1964

Roger Kochman, running back, Buffalo, 1963

Warren Koegel, center, Oakland, 1971, St. Louis, 1973, New York Jets, 1974

Larry Kubin, linebacker, Washington, 1981

Pete Kugler, defensive tackle, San Francisco, 1981

Ted Kwalick, tight end, San Francisco, 1969-74, Oakland, 1975-78

Ron LaPointe, tight end, Baltimore, 1980

Phil LaPorta, defensive tackle, New Orleans, 1974-75

Jim Laslavic, linebacker, Detroit, 1973-78, San Diego, 1979-81

Bill Lenkaitis, center, San Diego, 1968-70, New England, 1971-81

Pete Liske, quarterback, New York Jets, 1964, Denver, 1969-70, Philadelphia, 1971-72

Rich Lucas, defensive back, Buffalo, 1960-61

Len Luce, back, Washington, 1961

Roger Mahoney, center, Frankford, 1928-30, Minneapolis, 1930

Mark Markovich, guard, San Diego, 1974-75, Detroit, 1975-78

Rich Mauti, wide receiver, 1977-81

Mike McBath, defensive end, Buffalo, 1968-72

Ernest McCann, tackle, Hartford, 1926

Lance Mehl, linebacker, New York Jets, 1980-81

Lydell Mitchell, running back, Baltimore, 1972-77, San Diego, 1978-79, Los Angeles, 1980

Bob Mitinger, linebacker, San Diego, 1963-68

Mike Michalske, guard, New York Yankees, 1926-28, Green Bay, 1929-37

Matt Millen, linebacker, Oakland, 1980-81

Shorty Miller, quarterback, Massillon, 1919

Tom Mills, back, Green Bay, 1922-23

Rich Milot, linebacker, Washington, 1979-81

Booker Moore, fullback, Buffalo, 1981

Cliff Moore, back, Cincinnati, 1934

Red Moore, guard, Pittsburgh, 1947-49

Leo Nobile, guard, Washington, 1947, Pittsburgh, 1948-49

John Nolan, tackle, Boston, 1948, New York Bulldogs, 1949, New York Yankees, 1950

Al Olszewski, end, Pittsburgh, 1945

Ed O'Neil, linebacker, Detroit, 1974-81

Dennis Onkotz, linebacker, New York Jets, 1970

Robert Osborn, guard, Canton, 1921-23, Cleveland, 1924, Pottsville, 1925-28

Lou Palazzi, center, New York Giants, 1946-47

Mike Palm, quarterback, New York Giants, 1925-26, Cincinnati, 1933

Vic Panaccion, tackle, Frankford, 1930

Irv Pankey, tackle, Los Angeles, 1980-81

Bob Parsons, punter, Chicago, 1972-81
John Patrick, guard, Pittsburgh, 1941-46
John Petrella, back, Pittsburgh, 1945
Charlie Pittman, running back, St. Louis, 1970, Baltimore, 1971
Milt Plum, quarterback, Cleveland, 1957-61, Detroit, 1962-67, Los Angeles, 1968, New York Giants, 1969
William Pritchard, back, Providence, 1927, New York Yankees, 1928
Tom Rafferty, guard/center, Dallas, 1976-81
Richard Rauch, guard, Columbus, 1921, Toledo, 1922, Pottsville, 1925, New York Yankees, 1928, Boston Braves, 1929
Otis Redinger, back, Canton, 1925
Mike Reid, defensive tackle, 1970-74
George Reihner, guard, Houston, 1977-80
Glenn Ressler, guard, Baltimore, 1965-74
Bob Riggle, defensive back, Atlanta, 1966-67
Harry Robb, quarterback, Canton, 1921-23
Dave Robinson, linebacker, Green Bay, 1963-72, Washington, 1973-74
John Roepke, back, Frankford, 1928
Fran Rogel, running back, Pittsburgh, 1950-57
Hatch Rosedahl, defensive end, Buffalo, 1964, Kansas City, 1964-66
Dave Rowe, defensive tackle, New Orleans, 1967-70, New England, 1971-73, San Diego, 1974-75, Oakland, 1975-77, Baltimore, 1978-79
Bill Saul, linebacker, Baltimore, 1962-63, Pittsburgh, 1964-68, New Orleans, 1969, Detroit, 1970
Carl Schaukowitch, guard, Denver, 1975-77
Maury Schleicher, linebacker, San Diego, 1960-62
Richard Schuster, end, Canton, 1925
Bob Scrabis, QB, New York Jets, 1960-62
Tom Sherman, quarterback, New England, 1968-69, Buffalo, 1969
Mickey Shuler, tight end, New York Jets, 1978-80
Chuck Sieminski, defensive tackle, San Francisco, 1963-65, Atlanta, 1966-67, Detroit, 1968
John Skorupan, linebacker, Buffalo, 1973-77, New York Giants, 1978-80
George Snell, back, Brooklyn, 1926, Buffalo, 1927
Andy Stynchula, defensive lineman, Washington, 1960-63, New York Giants, 1964-65, Baltimore, 1966-67, Dallas, 1968
Matt Suhey, fullback, Chicago, 1980-81
Steve Suhey, guard, Pittsburgh, 1948-49
Sam Tamburo, end, New York Bulldogs, 1949
Jim Tays, back, Kansas City, 1924, Chicago Cardinals, 1925, Chicago Bulls, 1926, Dayton, 1927, Newark, 1930, Staten Island, 1930
William Thomas, back, Frankford, 1924, Philadelphia Quakers, 1926
Elgie Tobin, end, Akron, 1919-21

Bob Torrey, fullback, Miami, 1979, Philadelphia, 1980
Wally Triplett, back, Detroit, 1949-50, Chicago Cardinals, 1952-53
William Ullery, back, Dayton, 1922
Les Walters, end, Washington, 1958
Charlie Way, back, Canton 1921, Frankford, 1924, Philadelphia Quakers,
    1926
Bob Wear, center, Philadelphia, 1942
Byron Wontz, back, Pottsville, 1925-29
Gerald Wender, back, Buffalo, 1920
Howard Yerger, back, Dayton, 1919, Louisville, 1921